PRAISE FOR *WITH SIGNS FOLLOWING*

"This book clearly expands the current scholarship on the Church of God in Christ, arguably the world's fastest growing denomination. It contains much new information about the life, thought, and ministry of its founder, Charles Harrison Mason, as well as careful analyses of the church's theology, social witness, African roots, and impressive organizational structure for women's leadership that was made possible by the practical wisdom of its benevolent founder. Clergy, laity, seminarians, and scholars will find in this volume many new and challenging insights."

—PETER PARIS, PRINCETON THEOLOGICAL SEMINARY

"What a powerful, insightful book about Charles Harrison Mason. From a historical perspective, Dr. Raynard D. Smith provides a comprehensive immersion into the life and legacy of a great spiritual leader and founder of the Church of God in Christ (COGIC). Drawing from the collection of essays, Dr. Smith masterfully traces the complex yet complete account of Charles Harrison Mason's journey to establish the COGIC. According to Dr. Smith, this book introduces new information about Charles Harrison Mason–a religious African American icon. It is also one of the few revealing books that presents an accurate, well-documented portrayal of the events impacting the establishment and tremendous growth of the COGIC. A must-read for the religious community seeking truth!"

—WILLIE BRAGG, MORGAN STATE UNIVERSITY

"*With Signs Following* is well-researched, accessible, and engaging scholarship on Charles H. Mason, an influential black Pentecostal pioneer who founded the Church of God in Christ, the largest black Pentecostal denomination. It is a must-read and a gem for scholars, clergy, laity, and anyone seeking to enhance their understanding of Pentecostalism."

—JONATHAN L. CHISM, UNIVERSITY OF HOUSTON

"Dr. Smith presents a brilliant academic 'work of art' chronicling the life of the revered founder of the Church of God in Christ (COGIC), Charles Harrison Mason. By recapitulating Mason's life and legacy, Smith makes an important contribution to the scope of Mason's ministry specific to both clergymen and women. Unique to his ministry is the portrayal of how churchwomen, their work, and involvement within the denomination were embraced by Mason. Evidenced in his organizational structure and practice, his vision was a symbiotic model for ministry/leadership of both sexes. This work is grounded in select essays giving an in-depth examination of COGIC history and highlighting the birth of other churches which emerged from this congregation. This is a must-read for every COGIC member who is serious about empowering the next generation of church leaders with knowledge concerning their roots."

—Cynthia Bragg, Morgan State University, Baltimore

WITH *Signs* FOLLOWING

THE LIFE AND MINISTRY OF CHARLES HARRISON MASON

RAYNARD D. SMITH, EDITOR

ST. LOUIS, MISSOURI

Cover design: Michael T. Henderson, michaelthenderson.com.
Interior design: Crystal Devine

Print: 9780827243194 EPUB: 9780827243200 EPDF: 9780827243217

Library of Congress Cataloging-in-Publication Data

With signs following : the life and ministry of Charles Harrison Mason / Raynard D. Smith, editor. – First [edition].
pages cm
Includes bibliographical references and index.
ISBN 978-0-8272-4319-4 (pbk. : alk. paper) – ISBN 978-0-8272-4322-4 (hard-cover : alk. paper)
1. Mason, C. H. (Charles Harrison), 1866-1961. 2. Church of God in Christ–History. I. Smith, Raynard D., 1956- editor.
BX7056.Z8M379 2015
289.9'4092–dc23
[B]

2015033149

Dedication

This book is dedicated to the Late Bishop Ithiel Conrad Clemmons, COGIC's first historian.

Contents

About the Authors

Christopher Brennan (MLS, Academic Librarianship, State University of New York College at Geneseo) is the retired Director of Gardner A. Sage Library and Associate Professor of Theological Bibliography at New Brunswick Theological Seminary New Brunswick, N.J. He is a layperson in the Episcopal Church with twenty-five years of experience as a genealogist. His research contributed to the confirmation of the birth date of Bishop Charles Harrison Mason.

Ithiel C. Clemmons (DMin, New York Theological Seminary) was the Jurisdictional Bishop of Eastern New York First Jurisdiction and a member of the General Board of the Church of God in Christ. He was the denomination's first historian and served as the chairman of the executive committee of the Pentecostal/Charismatic Churches of North America (PCCNA) and past president of the Society for Pentecostal Studies (SPS).

David D. Daniels III (PhD, Church History, Union Theological Seminary, N.Y.) is Professor of Church History at McCormick Theological Seminary in Chicago. He is an Auxiliary Bishop and the director of the Board of Education in the Church of God in Christ. He is author of various articles on the history of Christianity and book reviews published in Theological Education in *Pneuma, Christian Century, Encyclopedia of African American Religions*, and *A Sourcebook for the Community of Religions.* He also served as an advisor to Legacy of a Leader, a 1991 video documentary on Charles Harrison Mason. He serves on the editorial committee of "A New History of World Christianity" project funded by Orbis Press.

Glenda Williams Goodson (MBA, Strategic Leadership, Amberton University, Tex.) is the founding director of The Center for African American Church History and Research, and an evangelist in the Church of God in Christ. She is a former journalist who writes professionally as an award-winning author of a number of books, including children's Christian activity books, history books, and biographies. Her published works include Royalty Unveiled–a five-year research study of COGIC international missionaries from 1920–1970–and biographies of Bishop A.T. Moore (*The Making of a Legend*) and Bishop J. N. Haynes (*The Appropriate Churchman*).

ROBERT R. OWENS (PhD, Organizational Leadership, Regent University, Va.) is Associate Professor of History at Southside Virginia Community College in Blackburn, Virginia. He is an ordained elder in the Pentecostal Holiness Church and the Church of God in Christ. He has published four books: *America Won the Vietnam War*, *Azusa Street Revival*, *Never Forget*, and *The Constitution Failed.*

CRAIG SCANDRETT-LEATHERMAN (PhD, Anthropology, University of Kansas) is co-founder of Faith for Justice in St. Louis, which encourages biblical activism and makes bridges between church and protest communities. He is an ordained minister in the Free Methodist Church. He has published several articles, including "Historic, Anthropological, and Afro-Pentecostal Perspectives on Black Manhood after 1865," in *Afro-Pentecostalism* (Yong & Alexander, eds.).

RAYNARD D. SMITH (PhD, Psychology and Religion, Drew University, N.J.) is Associate Professor of Pastoral Care/Pastoral Theology at New Brunswick Theological Seminary in New Brunswick, N.J. He is an ordained elder in the Church of God in Christ, the Coordinator of the COGIC Scholars Fellowship, editor of the COGIC Scholars newsletter (The Advocate), and a member of the COGIC Board of Education. He is the author of the forthcoming publication *Come Sunday Morning: Black Churches as Healing Communities.*

FREDERICK L. WARE (PhD, Religion, Vanderbilt University) is Associate Professor of Theology at Howard University School of Divinity. He is an ordained elder in the Church of God in Christ and has been active in ecumenical affairs, participating in dialogues of the international joint consultative group of Pentecostals and the World Council of Churches. He is author of *Methodologies of Black Theology* and the forthcoming textbook *African American Theology: An Introduction.* He has several published essays that explore the intersections of Pentecostalism with race, culture, healthcare, and the religion-science dialogue.

Acknowledgments

As the coordinator of the COGIC Scholars Fellowship, out of which this C.H. Mason book project is derived, I would like to express my gratitude to a host of persons and institutions that have supported our vision on this volume. I first express my appreciation for the late Bishop Ithiel Clemmons, to whom this volume is dedicated (and who is responsible for one of the chapters of this book). In addition, my deep appreciation goes to the other six authors who contributed essays to this volume for their scholarship, belief, and persistence in this project. I am grateful to the denomination, the Church of God in Christ (COGIC), Presiding Bishop Charles E. Blake Sr., and Dr. Alonzo Johnson who, while serving as the Dean of Education for the denomination early on, saw the significance of the creation of the COGIC Scholars Fellowship and provided us with a platform within the denomination for which to hold our academic forums during COGIC's Holy Convocation and Auxiliaries in Ministries (AIM) convention.

I am also grateful for the continuous support of Dr. Goldie Wells, Evangelist Sara Gooch, and Dr. Quintin Robertson of the O.T. Jones Sr. Institute for ensuring our inclusion in the workshop offerings during our denomination's annual Holy Convocation. Gratitude is also extended to the Deans of the leadership of the AIM Conventions who, over the years, ensured that our programming was included in the AIM booklet. In particular, I would like to thank Evangelist Jackie Jackson, Elder Keith Kershaw, and Auxiliary Bishop Willard Payton and all the people who worked in the "Command Central" for their consistent support.

Appreciation is due to The Society for Pentecostal Studies, where some of these essays were presented. And I owe a debt of gratitude to Dr. Harold Bennett and the C.H. Mason Theological Seminary of the Interdenominational Theological Center in Atlanta. I am also grateful to every person who has presented at the COGIC Scholars Fellowship Academic Forums over the fifteen years that we have been in existence. And I am grateful to the leadership who have provided me the relevant advice needed to appropriately guide the fellowship over the years: Evangelist Glenda Williams Goodson, Dr. Eric Greaux, Dr. Charles Hill, Elder Oscar Owens, and Dr. Eric Williams. I am deeply indebted to Evangelist Mary Lewis Freeman, who has served in the capacity of formatting the newsletter and has helped with the construction of the book cover.

In addition, I want to express my appreciation to the administration, faculty, staff, and students at New Brunswick Theological Seminary, who have in numerous ways served me as conversational partners and supporters on my quest to complete this project. In particular, I am indebted to Dr. Joanne Noel for her editorial skills, Jose A. Ebanks for his IT skills and assistance with formatting, and Tom Schlatter for his IT support.

And finally, I am tremendously grateful to my wife, Joanne, and family for allowing me to be absent from home in my quest to gather data or serve the church as the coordinator of COGIC Scholars Fellowship. And, to anyone whose name I may have forgotten to include here, I thank you for your support and prayers.

Introduction

Raynard D. Smith

In November 1981, at the 11th annual meeting of the Society for Pentecostal Studies, the late Ithiel Clemmons, a bishop in, and historian of, the Church of God in Christ (COGIC), who acquired his theological training at Union Theological Seminary in New York, said in his Presidential Address that the Society should strive for a more honest, nuanced, and inclusive conversation on the history of Pentecostalism that would include the contributions of African American leaders. Clemmons noted that leaders of significant Pentecostal denominations such as William J. Seymour, Charles Price Jones, Charles Harrison Mason, and Garfield T. Haywood, each of whom played pivotal roles in the propagation of the Pentecostal movement of the early twentieth century, were missing from the published Pentecostal histories due to what he identified as a neglect stemming from the racial attitudes that pervade the Pentecostal movement. Though Clemmons sleeps, his words of challenge to the Society have remained with me up to this time. Clemmons would later gift the church with a seminal text on Charles Harrison Mason and the Church of God in Christ in which he established key points: the cultural reservoir of slave religion that infused and informed Mason's ministry, an inclusive racial community that Mason envisioned, and the complementary role of women in ministry.

One response to Clemmons's challenge has been the formation of the COGIC Scholars Fellowship, a supportive academic network of scholars mostly, but not exclusively, within the Church of God in Christ. Since 2000, the COGIC Scholars Fellowship has held academic sessions at the Holy Convocation and Auxiliaries in Ministry Conference, two of the largest yearly COGIC conventions. Scholars both within and outside of the denomination have participated in these academic forums, sharing the distinctive perspective of their academic disciplines on the study of the Church of God in Christ, and C.H. Mason, and other important figures and issues within the denomination. The yields of these sessions have been rich, increasing the range and depth of interpretation on Mason and COGIC.

On the commemoration of Bishop Mason's one hundred and fiftieth year birthdate in 2014, it was felt that this information produced through the COGIC Scholars Fellowship finally needed to move to another level in which it could be shared with a larger audience than those in attendance at the academic sessions. The denomination founded and led by C.H. Mason is not only the largest Pentecostal denomination in the United States; it is also among the largest Protestant Christian denominations in the United States. There is increasing interest in COGIC, which was singularly shaped by Mason. It seemed appropriate to gather the papers presented at the academic forums and edit them for book publication. The scholarship presented at the COGIC Scholars meetings has been developed by scholars trained in a variety of disciplines: anthropology, sociology, theology, psychology, social ethics, and history. These papers have engendered much discussion and debate within the COGIC Scholars sessions and have substantially contributed to COGIC scholarship in particular, and African American religion and theology in general. It is with this acknowledgment that this collection of essays initially known as the C.H. Mason Book Project is set free through this publication.

The title of the C.H. Mason book project, *With Signs Following: The Life and Ministry of Charles Harrison Mason*, is inspired by Mason's frequent quotation of "And these signs shall follow them that believe..." (Mk. 16:17–18). The book is a collection of seven essays that were originally presented as papers at the COGIC Scholars Academic Forums from 2005 to 2014 present. Since the time of the last forum, the authors of the papers have revised and, in some cases, expanded their essays. Chapter 1, however, which introduces the collection of essays, is the original call for scholarship on Mason that Ithiel Clemmons gave in his Presidential Address to the Society for Pentecostal Studies meeting. Here Clemmons first sounded the clarion call for a more inclusive history on Mason and other African American Pentecostal leaders. I was able to obtain consent for this essay both from Clemmons's widow, Clara Clemmons, and the *Pneuma* journal in which it was first published in 1984.

In the second chapter, Christopher Brennan, the director of library services at New Brunswick Theological Seminary and a genealogist, brought his skills to bear as he has unearthed significant new census documents on the early life of Charles Harrison Mason and provided the scholarship on Mason and the denomination with a definitive date of Mason's birth in 1864, as well as other background information on Mason's family life. Trained as a genealogist and reference librarian, Brennan examines the extant sources on Mason to challenge some of the myths that have generally tended to surround his early life. He addresses questions of Mason's actual birth date, the mystery of Mason's family of origin, and the involvement of his father in the Civil War. Through his hard labor of unearthing census data and genealogical records, Brennan offers new credible conclusions that further our knowledge of Mason the person.

Chapter 3 is by Craig Scandrett-Leatherman. A trained anthropologist, Scandrett-Leatherman explores the connections of African religions with the contemporary expression of Afropentecostal religion as manifested in Mason's teachings and the Church of God in Christ. Scandrett-Leatherman argues that Mason's yearning for the power of slave religion, and his incorporation of the practices of drums and dance, demonstrate that Mason drew upon African roots. He contends that numerous COGIC rituals and social practices show continuity with African practices and discontinuity with European and Native American practices.

The fourth chapter is written by Frederick Ware. Ware brings the perspective of theology and culture. His essay examines Mason's use and understanding of signs within the context of the American South at the beginning of the twentieth century, and the biblical basis for signs in Pentecostal theology. Ware contends Mason preached using natural objects and events as signs mediating deep spiritual truths. The use of signs in Mason's preaching to an agrarian population in the early twentieth century was a medium to effectively communicate the Bible within an overwhelmingly illiterate population. Ware's essay serves as a corrective to those who have interpreted Mason's use of objects as dabbling in conjure (magic), occult, or demonic. Ware asserts that Mason's use of "freaks of nature" was solely to convey spiritual truths from the Bible.

The fifth chapter is written by Robert Owens. From the perspective of a historian, Owens' essay advances the theory that Mason was the "Apostle of Reconciliation" within the early Pentecostal movement. Owens argues that Mason's ministry had a key role in the reconciliation of the races and fostered an atmosphere of love and acceptance that has had a lasting effect upon the Christian church in America. Owens draws upon primary sources–in particular, little-known books and articles self-published by Church of God in Christ members , to construct a convincing argument in favor of Mason's racially inclusive vision. Using the critical investigation of a professional historian, this essay reveals several little-known aspects of COGIC history and Mason's ministry of reconciliation.

The sixth chapter, written by Glenda Williams Goodson, turns the focus of the essays to a nuanced interpretation of Mason's interaction with women in ministry. Drawing upon historical records of women's biographies, Goodson argues that despite COGIC's policy against women's ordination, Mason was an advocate for women in ministry. Though Mason did not ordain, he did not hinder women and thus recognized their complementary role in the work of salvation and the expansion of the church.

The seventh chapter is my contribution to the Mason discourse. Trained in psychology of religion and ethics, I attempt to bring a psycho-social-ethical perspective to my essay as it looks at the way in which Mason, both as a religious leader and American citizen, addressed the issue of racism during his time. This essay contends that Mason built a ministry of spiritual and social uplift among ex-slaves and their descendants. It explores Mason's leadership style, in particular as he addressed the racial issues of the socio-political climate in which he lived and did ministry. It contends that Mason operated within a dialectical tension embodying the priestly/pastoral and the prophetic leadership styles that extend back to the coast of Africa. It sees this stream of social consciousness with the tradition to this day.

Finally, the eighth chapter is written by David Douglas Daniels III, who is the premier scholar on COGIC history. Trained in American religious history, Daniels situates Mason as a folk or organic theologian who seeks to communicate the Christian faith in "plain words for plain people." He notes that Mason engaged in a theological reflection that was "practical and occasional rather than theoretical and systematic." He contends that Mason's theological journey has left an indelible imprint on the doctrine of the Church of God in Christ, and paved a theological trajectory within North American Pentecostalism that has had an immense impact on the Black Church throughout the twentieth century.

In this collection of essays, readers will find that there is a continuous thread that runs throughout. This thread is the rich African cultural heritage out of which Mason operated and which continues to influence the denomination. In addition, this collection of essays brings new information concerning Mason and the COGIC to the fore. Through this collection of essays, written by scholars well versed in their particular disciplines, the historical antecedents for Mason's lineage (as far back as slavery) are established: his connection with his African heritage is maintained, Mason's leadership style is explored, his integration of agrarian society into his preaching style is examined, his treatment of women as partners in ministry is nuanced, and the psychosocial impact of his environment upon his socio-ethical views on racism are highlighted.

While a few very good books have been written on the institutional culture of COGIC, this collection of essays differs in that each essay begins with Mason as its central focus and brings an analytical gaze from a particular discipline upon a key central aspect of his life and ministry and the implications of both for the development of COGIC. Other excellent books on COGIC include: Ithiel Clemmons' *Bishop C.H. Mason and the Roots of the Church of God in Christ* (Pneuma Press, 1997); Anthea Butler's *Women in the Church of God in Christ: Making a Sanctified World* (University of North Carolina Press, 2007); Calvin White Jr.'s *The Rise to Respectability: Race, Religion, and the Church of God in Christ* (University of Arkansas Press, 2012); and Richard Pitt's *Divine Callings: Understanding the Call to Ministry in Black Pentecostalism* (New York University Press, 2012). In contrast to these books, the analytical perspectives of this collection of essays include exploration of Mason's connection with his African cultural heritage, his leadership style, his use of symbols in his preaching delivery, his approach to racism, and more.

It is envisioned that this collection of essays will appeal to several audiences and accordingly have many uses. This rich collection of scholarly essays on Mason will have a wide appeal to scholars of Southern history and culture, and American religious history and the Black Church; religion scholars of Holiness and Pentecostal traditions; scholars of Black religion; as well as the leadership and laity of the COGIC denomination. Religion scholars should have a particular interest in Mason and the COGIC due to the fact that the denomination that he founded at the turn of the century (1897–1907) has continued to grow into a major Black Church tradition with a membership exceeding 4 million and is now in its one hundred and seventh year of existence. The success of this denomination is established in Robert Owen's essay in chapter 5.

The COGIC is in the process of establishing required training for its entire clergy seeking ordination. This collection of essays will serve well in providing candidates for ordination with substantial knowledge of the founder and his theology. It could be envisioned that this collection of essays could become a major text used by the ordination committees as COGIC seeks to standardize the training process of its ordained clergy. In addition, this collection will also appeal to laity who have an interest in the life of the founder and the development of COGIC. But, most importantly, this collection of essays on Mason will allow another generation of people, in particular youth, removed from Mason's time and era to read about a man who was a product of his time but who overcame many obstacles of poverty, racism, and classism to achieve a level of greatness unsurpassed by his peers. It is with this understanding that I am pleased to release these essays to the larger public.

1

TRUE KOINONIA

Pentecostal Hopes and Historical Realities

ITHIEL C. CLEMMONS[1]

Beloved colleagues, brothers and sisters, it has been a great privilege for me to serve this year as President of so distinguished an association of scholars as the Society for Pentecostal Studies. I am doubly honored to have been called upon to serve during the 75th Anniversary of the Azusa Revival–a revival that has come to be viewed as a major American contribution to Christianity.[2]

The Society for Pentecostal Studies traces its beginning to that 20th Century Awakening. Pentecostalism's phenomenal spread in this century, with its claims to valid primitive Christianity, its challenges to traditional Christian Faith, and its contribution to Protestant, Catholic, and Eastern Orthodox Church renewal accounts for an estimated 35–50 million adherents around the world. This is indeed one of the fascinating aspects of recent Church history.

I assumed the mantle of presidency of this august body with some trepidation.[3] But, not being one who succumbs to fear and trembling or backs away from ideological encounter, the year has provided me an opportunity to search for previously undisclosed primary source material, to reassess some commonly held views that have proven inadequate in light of these new source materials, and to press for a closing of the conscious and unconscious gaps that exist in our knowledge about the founders of this revolutionary Christian Movement.[4]

This evening, I want to lift up the contribution of just one of the founders of the 20th Century Pentecostal Movement who has been shamefully neglected in Pentecostal historiography in general.

I wish to do this for two reasons: First, the most obvious, is that Bishop Charles Harrison Mason, founder of the Church of God in Christ, is the focus of my own doctoral studies and it makes practical sense for me to hold to my area of deepest preoccupations. Second, the shameful neglect of such Pentecostal giants as C.H. Mason, W.J. Seymour, and G.T. Haywood is reflective of a mind-set that has informed Pentecostal historiography from its very beginning that we must deal with honestly, in the love of Christ, before the veracity of Pentecostal origins can be adequately established and before the Pentecostal bodies that have emerged over these 75 years can fulfill their raison d'être.

The original vision has been lost largely because the Black pioneers of the Pentecostal Movement have been shamefully neglected. Modern church history needs to close this gap created by historical racism.

Before summarizing and looking at the basic contributions of Charles Harrison Mason, I want to call attention to three literary works that have attended the diamond jubilee of the Azusa Revival. Two of these works relate directly to the central point that I seek to make in this address. These works are: (1) Frank Bartleman, *Azusa Street*, foreword by Vinson Synan (Plainfield, N.J.: Logos International, 1980), a republication of *How Pentecost Came to Los Angeles*, a personal diary published by Bartleman in 1925, three years after Seymour's death; (2) Dr. Douglas J. Nelson, "For Such a Time as This: The Story of Bishop William J. Seymour, A Search for Pentecostal/Charismatic Roots," a doctoral dissertation completed for the Theology Department (University of Birmingham at Birmingham, England, May 1981); and (3) Kilian McDonnell, OSB, STD, ed., *Presence, Power, Praise: Documents on the Charismatic Renewal*, 3 vols., (Collegeville, Minn.: Liturgical Press, 1980). This is Father McDonnell's Magnum Opus of the Charismatic Movement.

My distinguished colleague, Dr. Vinson Synan, is to be commended for his enlightening introduction to Frank Bartleman's diary. It is extremely helpful, especially to those who have not read Frank Bartleman's story in *From Plow to Pulpit*. It helps us to get a portrait of the man. Bartleman, in 1925, two decades following the watershed revival, seeks to recall those early days in an effort to answer the question, the deep sigh of many of the old timers, "What happened to the glory?" Bartleman's attempt to answer the question has bequeathed to us a valuable account of the religious milieu that formed the social and religious context of the revival.

With the new research tools (e.g., Erikson's psychohistory) that we have available for historical interpretation today, we are able to better understand Bartleman as a man of his times and to more accurately evaluate the reliability of his duty. His life seemed over-beset by poverty and misfortune. Times were hard for him and he was given to bouts of deep depression. The sainted Ruth Fisher perceived him as a man who walked with his head in a cloud. I suppose it is not difficult to belittle such an impractical person. Yet, he was a deeply sensitive spirit whose attachment to a hidden world of the spirit was overwhelming, whose sense of the transcendent sustained his soul and thrust him beyond the immediate purposes of livelihood. He received brilliant flashes of historical and spiritual insight. The following is but one such gestalt observation:

We had been called to bless and serve the whole body of Christ, everywhere Christ is one, and his "body" can be but "one." We were all baptized into one body. (I Cor. 12:12). The church is an organism not a human organization.[5]

In brilliant flashes of insight, he could perceive the moments when the divine-human encounter transcended the entrapment of social categories of class and caste. Yet, alas, like his brethren from B.F. Lawrence[6] to Robert Mapes Anderson,[7] with few exceptions (Hollenweger, Lovett, Tinney, Synan, Menzies, Nelson), he was so bound to the social a priori of White culture that the tremendous contributions of people of color to the Movement was at best peripheral. Even when these spiritual and ecclesiastical giants were perceived as "eleventh hour comers to the movement," their genius was seen as derived from White culture rather than from divine revelation. This is not a chauvinistic or cavalier put-down of my colleagues in the fields of Pentecostal theology and history. This is rather a conclusion drawn from a careful reading of the literature. How else does one interpret Bartleman's insight that "the color line was washed away in the blood" (p. 54) and yet, be so blind to W.H. Durham's divisive activities? How else could Bartleman so completely gloss over Clara Lum's stealing of the *Apostolic Faith Newspaper*, an event that marked the beginning of the end of the revival? Bartleman is indeed a valuable source for understanding the readiness of Los Angeles for the revolutionary spiritual movement, but save for brief flashes of exceptional insight, he is, for the most part, unreliable as a historian of the movement because of his obvious entrapment in social a priori White categories, despite his spiritual sensitivity.

The social a priori of White culture that informed and continues to inform particular White theologians and historians of the Pentecostal Movement is especially revealed in the intensified and renewed drive since the 1950s to hail Charles Fox Parham as the Father of the contemporary Pentecostal Movement at the expense of William J. Seymour, the man whom God truly used. This is due not so much to devious intention of particular theologians and historians as it is to the social context in which their thinking occurs. It is an expression of two centuries of English Protestant theology that, as Peter Gay has so perceptively observed, "gives God His glory, assigns men their places, gives events their meaning-and Anglo-Saxon superiority its due."[8] It is unfortunate that, in telling this marvelous story of Pentecostal origins in America, these brilliant chroniclers have become so enclosed within their own social contexts that they are lured to treat their distorted visions of reality as the whole truth. And they feel they must destroy other stories that bear witness that the history of the movement can be seen from another perspective.

Fortunately, this 75th Anniversary of the Azusa Street Revival has called forth a study that is destined to be one of the most significant works on Modern Pentecostal origins ever produced. Historians inside and outside the Movement have had little interest in an accurate account of Bishop W. J. Seymour, notwithstanding his crucial significance. Walter Hollenweger, in a personal communication to me this past summer, wrote of Dr. Douglas J. Nelson's doctoral dissertation:

> ...Doug Nelson has convincingly shown that without William J. Seymour, there would have undoubtedly been some form of revival as America has had many, but nothing compared to what the Pentecostal revival is about.[9]

Nelson has convincingly argued that William J. Seymour's Azusa Mission represented the restoration of human equality in the body of Christ for the first time since the first Christian Pentecost and early Christianity. Seymour's leadership gave something to Western European civilization, something that was missing–and since has been rejected and remains lost. Seymour brought together the apostolic vision of "beloved community" of human equality. Seymour championed one doctrine above all others: There must be no color line or any other division in the Church of Jesus Christ because God is no respecter of persons. This inclusive fellowship is not a human construct but a divine glossolalia community of human equality. Spiritual power sprang more from interracial equality than from glossolalia.[10] "As long as the practice of glossolalia remains alienated from its roots in Christian oneness beyond the color line, it must be at best socially irrelevant. To be genuinely Christian, it requires expression within the larger social vision of its historic roots."[11]

Nelson is a White American clergyman of the United Methodist Church, a retired Chaplain (LTC) U.S. Army, who since 1975 has been an interested participant in the Pentecostal/Charismatic Movement. Nelson's study is significant because for the first time in the twentieth century, we are presented with a full, detailed, accurate portrait of the leader of the Azusa Revival. Moreover, for the first time, we are able to see fully what that revival was about from Seymour's perspective. Other writers, such as Brumback,[12] have indeed devoted considerable attention to Seymour and Azusa Mission, along with a thorough analysis of the Pentecostal Movement. Nelson is not the first to hold up the interracial element. He is the first, however, to grasp the connection between glossolalia and the inclusive, interracial, egalitarian fellowship as being all-important and the source of that revival's powerful attention. Nelson's evidence is so overwhelming as to prompt Professor James Cone to say to me after reading his study: "The histories are going to have to be rewritten."[13] Here is the story of a people in a situation of dialectic encounter with an Other wherein they are grasped by the One who is other than self. Truth in this sense was not derived from human consciousness. Truth in this context was an event that occurred to people often against the human will, bringing about a true koinonia.[14] Faith for these people was not simply a feeling of inwardness separated from the historical struggle. Faith became an event that transcended, challenged, and transformed the social context.

If Nelson is true (and his evidence, drawn from heretofore overlooked primary materials, is overwhelming), past conclusions must be called into account as inadequate. We are now able to correct those caricatures of this morally impeccable Christian leader whom historical racism has caused to be shamefully portrayed.[15]

Nelson's finding corroborates my own research based on other primary source materials heretofore overlooked. Even more than Seymour, Charles Harrison Mason has been heretofore shamefully neglected and underestimated, despite his importance in the origin, rise, and spread of the Pentecostal Movement. It was C.H. Mason, not C.F. Parham, who grasped and stood with Seymour in the revival that united glossolalia with Pauline vision of an all-inclusive egalitarian fellowship in which there is "...neither Jew nor Greek, bond nor free...male nor female..."(Gal. 3:28, Col. 3:11). Early twentieth-century America did not have the social fabric that could bind a fellowship that transcended race and class. The dream was certainly in accord with the American dream. But its radical, racial, egalitarian praxis challenged the racist presupposition of American society. Mason and Seymour stood together in this Pauline vision overlooked by White America, but created and nurtured in American slavery's "Invisible Institution" like diamond deep in the earth where enormous pressure bears on black anthracite coal.

Primary source material reveals that C.H. Mason and C.P. Jones influenced W.J. Seymour before he met Charles Fox Parham at Houston in August, 1905,[16] and that Mason's seminal supportive influence was a continual source of strength for him until his death in September 1922. Mason's significance went far beyond giving legal ecclesiastical status to independent clergy so that they could perform ministerial functions and receive reduced clergy rates on the nation's railroads (as historians have pointed out). Mason brought to the movement a combination of charismatic gifts and ecclesiastical churchmanship that gave the fledgling movement strength to endure despite efforts by insiders (Parham) and outsiders (*L. A. Times*) to crush it. While leaders A.J. Tomlinson and J.H. King, fast friends of Mason's, refused to attend the organizing meeting of the Assemblies of God in 1914 because of doctrinal differences, Mason, although overlooked by those who sent out letters announcing the meeting, chose to attend anyway, prayed for the brethren, and bade them God's speed. He was committed to Pentecostalism's primary vision of healing divisions. Yet he was wise enough to know that Blacks would always be constricted with Whites in leadership. Whites would allow doctrinal differences to break fellowship. Mason recognized doctrinal differences, retained their significance, but would not allow these differences to stand in the way of fellowship.

Seymour and Haywood both died at age 52, in 1922 and 1932, respectively. Evidence is that they both died of broken hearts brought on by resurgent racial attitudes in America. When White leaders tragically locked the Pentecostal Movement behind walls of race and class, Mason endured and upheld the radical spiritual and social vision of the Azusa Revival. He refused to divorce glossolalia and koinonia. He lived as a leader, an apostle, and ecclesiastical statesman.

One of the earliest White holiness-pentecostal converts wrote of the tremendous influence of C.H. Mason on his life and thinking, as well as on the lives of thousands of others Whites, as well as Blacks.[17] He wrote:

> I first met...Mason and C.P. Jones...at Conway, Arkansas, on the 19th day of November, 1904. I had only been preaching a little over a year. I was walking down the street at Conway, and I heard someone preaching. I was several blocks away and something said to me, "There is a public sale on and the auctioneer is speaking pretty loud." As I walked on towards the gathering, I was soon convinced that it was not a public sale; that it was preaching by a colored man. When I arrived, I found two or three thousand people standing around a cotton wagon in which Brother Mason stood preaching. At the conclusion of the sermon, Brother C.P. Jones, who was also in the wagon, sang two songs; one entitled, "Take Your Burdens to the Lord and Leave Them There," and the other, "I Am Happy With Jesus Alone, Though Poor and Deserted, Thank God I Can Say, I'm Happy With Jesus Alone..."
>
> The sermon and songs held the crown spellbound for something like an hour and a half, after I arrived. That day Brother Mason made an impression on me that I have never forgotten and can never forget... I doubt if there has ever been a minister who has lived since the day of the Apostles who has shown the sweet spirit to all people regardless of race, creed or color or has preached with greater power..."
>
> "In 1916, he conducted a great camp meeting for the Whites of Nashville, Tennessee, where more than 7,000 attended each night. I...heard of the highest politicians of America speak complimentary of Bishop Mason... I heard leaders of several organization say: "If Brother Mason was a White man we would gladly step aside our organizations."
>
> "Right here I wish to say the spirit of looking at color lines and not looking at the lowly Nazarene has and is sapping the real joy out of many Holiness and Pentecostal Movements of modern days."[18]

In 1952, at 86 years of age, C.H. Mason was at the World Pentecostal Conference in London, England, praising God and blessing the people. He lived longer than any founder of a major denomination in America. My father, Bishop Frank Clemmons, met Bishop W.J. Seymour in Harlem on Seymour's last trip East before his death. At the corner of 135th Street and Lenox Avenue in Harlem, W.J. Seymour asked him if he was acquainted with C.H. Mason. My father replied, "Yes, as a matter of fact, Bishop Mason is in New Jersey now attending a meeting." Seymour asked my father if it was possible for him to get with Brother Mason. My father took William J. Seymour to East Orange, New Jersey, to the home of Elder James Wells, Pastor of the Old Tabernacle Church of God in Christ. There my father witnessed the moving scene of C.H. Mason and W.J. Seymour weeping on each other's shoulders and praising God in power and glory. This was in the early 1920s (1921–1922); Mason and Seymour were close.

It was Mason to whom Seymour had turned for advice about marriage in 1908. C.H. Mason told me as we traveled together by train from Baltimore, Maryland, to New York City in 1952 that he warned Seymour against possible interracial marriage that might have been suggested, given the makeup of his congregation. Seymour followed Mason's advice. The rest is carefully documented by Nelson. When Mason passed away, on November 17, 1961, he and Seymour had bequeathed to the Christian Church a unique Pentecostal spirituality.

A community of the Spirit transcending class and caste was the original driving vision of Pentecostalism–a vision as sweeping and as powerful as was the Puritan vision of a Christian America. Like that Puritan-Evangelical vision of which it is part, the Pentecostal vision, though numerically and materially successful in tight, closed, country club caste of wealth and power, is still a victim of its loss of distinctive character. The true koinonia for which the world so desperately longs and awaits has slipped from its grasp.

Bishop William Joseph Seymour pointed the way to the beloved community and died. Bishop Charles Harrison Mason gave the fragmented community enduring significance. The fact that Seymour and Mason were both Black Americans caused them to be shamefully neglected. But their vision of a glossolalic-inclusive New Testament koinonia still remains a challenge to the modern church. These giants can be neglected, but they cannot be ignored.

2

When in the Course of Human Events?

Conflicting Indirect Evidence for the Birth and Paternity of Charles Harrison Mason

Christopher Brennan

The Problem

In 1860 the total slave population of the United States came to nearly 4 million persons.[1] After the Civil War ended in 1865, the former slaves had nothing to fall back on because nothing but freedom had been given. Most fell back into patterns they knew (e.g., working as household help or as tenant farmers for their former masters) and fell into obscurity, undisturbed by the efforts of historians, biographers, or genealogists.

A select few continue to pique our interest, either through their own accomplishments (e.g., abolitionist Frederick Douglass, Underground Railroad conductor Harriett Tubman, etc.) or through those of their progeny. One example of the latter is Jerry Mason, a former slave who would have died in obscurity except for the subsequent fame of one of his sons: Charles Harrison ("C.H.") Mason, revered as the founder of the Christian denomination known as the Church of God in Christ (COGIC). Although hard statistics are difficult to come by, COGIC itself claims to be one of the largest Black Pentecostal bodies in the country, with over 6 million members.[2]

Although regarded by his followers as the founder of a major Christian body, direct evidence for the birth and paternity of Charles Harrison Mason is lacking. The southern states most commonly associated with C.H. Mason's early life–Tennessee and Arkansas–did not register births until much later. Tennessee did not register births until 1908,[3] and Arkansas not until 1914.[4] A few communities have earlier records. For example, in Tennessee some records exist in Memphis from 1874, in Chattanooga from 1879, and Knoxville and Nashville from 1881.[5] In Arkansas some records exist from Fort Smith and Little Rock from 1881.[6] All of these records would be too late for Mason's purported birth.

C.H. Mason died 17 November 1961.[7] The informant for the personal information on his death certificate was his widow, Elsie (Washington) Mason (3 April 1907–January 31, 2006),[8] and she said Mason was born 8 September 1856, making him 105 years old at his death. His parents are given as: "Father unknown" and "Eliza (unknown)."[9] The omission of his father's name suggests either that she did not know it or that she could not remember the details.

Other members of the family claim a different date. His daughter Mary Mason claimed he was born 8 September 1866, the son of Jerry and Eliza Mason.[10] Other family members, while also claiming Jerry and Eliza Mason as his parents, attest that Mason claimed to be born two or three years before the end of the Civil War (suggesting a birth date of 1862 or 1863).[11] According to Arkansas historian Calvin White, 1862 is the birth year claimed by a historic marker at 930 Mason Street in Memphis, COGIC's national headquarters,[12] and at the time of his passing newspapers tributes gave his age as 98,[13] which would appear to support the 1862 or 1863 dates.

Nor is the problem accurately identifying Mason's birth limited to Charles Harrison Mason himself. For family members who do recall something of Mason's parents, there are contradictory accounts of when and where his father, Jerry Mason, died. For example, in the book entitled *From Prior's Farm to Heaven*–written by church elder Jack Hunt, but informed by Mason's daughter Leila (Mason) Byas (5 October 1910–20 December 2004)[14]–an account is given of the death of father Jerry Mason in the massacre that followed the Battle of Fort Pillow in 1864.[15] Other accounts suggest that Jerry Mason died of yellow fever in 1879, shortly after the family moved to Arkansas.[16]

EVIDENTIARY ISSUES

Given the contradiction in the family oral tradition, one would naturally want to turn to the contemporary evidence for resolution of the question; however, as noted, no contemporary certificate exists for C.H. Mason's birth. The next most logical source would be church records, but that too is problematic. Family oral tradition maintains that Mason's parents were Missionary Baptists, and Baptists of all stripes do not believe in infant baptism. Only those old enough to make their own commitment to the faith would be baptized, and the church records would only testify to the person being baptized and the date the rite took place. No information on the date of birth or the parents of the baptized would be provided.[17] Despite this, efforts *were* made to locate baptismal records for Charles Harrison Mason, to situate the family in a particular point in time and space, as well as confirm the conversion narrative passed down through the oral tradition. After diligent searching, it appears the records are not extant.

Thus the researcher is forced to seek indirect evidence for the birth and parents of Charles Harrison Mason. In an effort to uncover what Mason himself believed were the details of his birth, a request for his SS-5 (Application for a Social Security Account number) was submitted. In a 6 September 2012 letter, the Executive Director of the Office of Privacy and Disclosure indicated Social Security personnel were "unable to locate any record for Mr. Mason." This is not surprising, as clergy were ineligible for Social Security until 1955.[18] Given that he would probably have been in his eighties or early nineties by that date, it appears probable he never applied for a card.

One form he did complete was his application for a marriage license to Alice R. Saxton, 13 January 1890. In the marriage affidavit he attests to being 23 years old.[19] Assuming a September birthday, that means his last birthday was in September 1889 (and a likely birth date of September 1866). The datum, while helpful in acknowledging what C.H. Mason believed was his birthday, is not definitive. There is no specific date, location, nor information on his parents. More importantly, there is no available confirmation of that date. No one is a competent witness to his/her own birth. There are numerous instances in which a person believed the day, month, and year of their birth was a given, only to discover otherwise later. A famous instance is that of jazz trumpeter Louis Armstrong, who for years claimed he was born 4 July 1900, only to discover years later he was born 13 months later, 4 August 1901.[20] Documentary evidence closer to his birth needed to be found to confirm or disprove Charles Harrison Mason's own assumptions.

So the best source appears to be the census data, but for whom should one look? If Jerry Mason was a slave in 1860 and if his son Charles was born in 1856–as Charles' widow believed–father and son would be hard to find without knowledge of their owner's name. Slave schedules commonly listed slaves under the owner's name, and then only as "Black male" or "Black female" and their age. We will discuss later how uncertain age data are.

The 1870 U.S. census is a possible place to find this data, but if Jerry died at Fort Pillow (12 April 1864), he would not have been alive for the decennial enumeration, with the result being that we would need to seek Eliza's entry, either as a widow or with another husband. If Jerry did not die at Fort Pillow, he could have still been alive in 1870, presumably with his wife and children. So, the first question we need to answer is, "Did Jerry Mason die at Fort Pillow?"

THE FORT PILLOW MASSACRE

Before we get to the issue of Jerry Mason's service, it may be helpful to paint a general picture of what happened at Fort Pillow, and why it matters whether Jerry Mason served there or not. Tennessee was an active battleground during the Civil War, and among the most feared Confederate commanders was Nathan Bedford Forrest (13 July 1821–29 October 1877), who commanded his own cavalry corps. On 4 April 1864, Forrest writes from Jackson, Tennessee, to General Samuel Cooper (Confederate States' Adjutant and Inspector General) indicating that he (Forrest) plans to attack Fort Pillow, which has horses and supplies that are badly needed.[21] On the morning of 12 April 1864, he attacked the fort following a request of surrender that the Union commander refused. The battle commenced and the fort was overrun.[22]

But this only tells half the story. Union survivors told horrendous stories of what happened after the fort was taken. According to these accounts, after the battle had ended and Union soldiers were surrendering, both White and Black soldiers were slaughtered without mercy. Some were shot in cold blood. Some were run through with swords.[23] Some ran down to the river, seeking to escape and were either shot or drowned.[24] Of the 300 dead, almost two-thirds of that total, 192, were Black soldiers,[25] who seemed to be especially marked for death. Of the 213 Union soldiers captured, only 56 were Black. In contrast, 157 White soldiers were taken as prisoners.[26] The massacre would haunt Forrest and color his reputation, North and South, for the rest of his life.

Was Jerry Mason at Fort Pillow?

So, if Jerry Mason had served at Fort Pillow, the odds suggest he would have been among the dead, and Charles Harrison Mason would have grown up without a father (or not been born at all, depending on his date of birth). Blacks were not enrolled in the Union Army until after the preliminary Emancipation Proclamation in September 1862. Even after that date, most did not see action until after August 1863, by which time 14 Black regiments were in the field. Collectively, these segregated units were known as the United States Colored Troops (USCT).[27] To determine if Jerry served at Fort Pillow, we need to determine which units of the United States Colored Troops were stationed at the fort the day of the attack, 12 April 1864.

There were two units of the USCT at Fort Pillow: Battery D of the 2nd United States Colored Light Artillery, and the 6th United States Colored Heavy Artillery (the 1st Battalion).[28] A search was undertaken within these units to determine the presence of any soldier named Jerry Mason. The 6th had no Masons listed at all, while the 2nd had just one–James Mason. Absolutely no Jerry Mason was to be found. From the available evidence, Jerry was not there. This is not to suggest that Jerry did not serve. There are two units of United States Colored Troops with a "Jerry Mason"–the 12th Regiment of the United States Heavy Artillery, and the 44th United States Colored Infantry, Co. K. Of the two, the 44th is more likely the unit with which he served. The 12th was stationed exclusively in Kentucky from 1864 to 1866, and we have no indication our Jerry Mason had any connection to Kentucky.[29] On the other hand, the 44th was a Tennessee-based unit, and Mason family tradition strongly associates Jerry Mason with Tennessee. The 44th was organized 7 April 1864, but initially served garrison and desk duty at Chattanooga. Afterward, it saw action at Dalton, Georgia (13 October 1864), at the Battle of Nashville (15–16 December 1864), and pursued Confederate General John Bell Hood's forces to the Tennessee River (17–18 December 1864). Following that, the unit once more assumed post and garrison duty at Chattanooga until mustered out 30 April 1866.[30] If this was Jerry Mason's unit, he was involved in the battle at Dalton, Georgia, and was taken as a prisoner of war. According to the military records that do survive, his enrollment papers were lost in capture. He was dropped from the units rolls, so no further details about his military career are available.[31]

While it is commonly believed that Black soldiers were executed following capture, such was not the case universally. While it is true that such soldiers were not given the same treatment as their White counterparts, it was not a blanket Confederate policy to execute them. In many cases Black soldiers were either returned to their White owners (if such could be identified) or they were put to work by the Confederate government.[32] In the aftermath of the Battle of Dalton, the captured Colored Troops were put to work laboring for the defense of Mobile, Alabama. Several issues of the *Mobile Advertiser and Register* newspaper in 1864 reportedly testified to this, publishing the names of over 1300 Colored Troop prisoners put to work on the city's defenses.[33] Despite repeated efforts to obtain copies of the relevant issues, to determine if Jerry Mason's name was listed among the captured troops, the search was fruitless; evidently those issues are no longer extant.

Jerry Mason and Eliza Mason's Marriage and Residence

The family oral tradition suggests that Jerry and Eliza lived in Shelby County, Tennessee (near Memphis), and after the war Charles Harrison Mason grew up on "the Prior Farm," outside Memphis.[34] Contemporary evidence supports this assertion, as records indicate two Blacks named Jerry and Eliza Mason were living in Shelby County, Tennessee, after the war. The Freedmen's Bureau records document that Jerry Mason and Eliza Mason wed 17 September 1865 in Memphis, Tennessee. Both were from Memphis, were Black and 35 years old (meaning they were born sometime around 1830). They had been living together for three years before the marriage and together had three children.[35] If this sounds strange to modern ears, that two reputedly religious individuals in nineteenth-century America should have several children out of wedlock, it should be noted that slave marriage had no legal standing in southern states. Spouses could be separated at any time the owner willed, such that many slave marriages before 1865 consisted of little more than the couple moving into a cabin together (and then only if the owner approved).[36]

The Freedmen's Bureau believed they had no children apart from their relationship.[37] As we will see below, the latter detail likely is not true, but the Freedmen's record *does* support their marriage.

Census Records Relating to Charles Harrison Mason

The first census in which the whole family would be featured, therefore, is the 1870 return for Shelby County. In it we find a family headed by a man named "Cherry Mason," a 45-year-old Black male farm laborer. Also listed with him is his wife Eliza Mason (a 43-year-old Black female who kept house), and their seven children: Israel Mason (18-year-old male); Joe Mason (16-year-old male); Elsy [sic] Mason (6-year-old female); Mary Mason (12-year-old female); Charley Mason (5-year-old male); Jerry Mason (4-year-old male); and Robert Mason (the youngest child, aged 2/12 [2 months]).[38]

The ages subtracted from the census year (1870) yield the following estimated dates of birth:

- Cherry Mason 1824/25
- Eliza Mason 1826/27
- Israel Mason 1851/52
- Joe Mason 1853/54
- Mary Mason 1857/58
- Elsy Mason 1863/64
- Charley Mason 1864/65
- Jerry Mason 1865/66
- Robert Mason April 1870

We can be more exact for Robert as his age is given as two months. The census taker visited the family June 24, 1870. Two months before June gives an estimated birthdate of April 1870 (which is also explicitly noted in the return).[39]

The census also tells us that both parents were born in Virginia, all the children were born in Tennessee, neither parent could read or write, and all the children were still at home.[40] Before we draw any hasty conclusions, let us bring in a complicating factor, that of the following census, the 1880 United States Census. The family oral tradition, as recounted in Mary Mason's biography of her father, indicate the family should have been in Plumerville (Conway County), Arkansas at that time.[41] As noted, some strands of the oral tradition suggest Jerry had died by 1880,[42] but even if that is the case, Eliza and the children would have still been there somewhere.

Plumerville was a village in the Town of Howard, Arkansas, and there clearly was an African American family named Mason living in the area, although in 1880 both parents were very much alive. This family was headed by a man named Jeremiah Mason (66 years old and a farmer), and his wife Eliza Mason (56 years old and keeping house). The children present include: Eliza Mason (16 years old, at home); Charles Mason (14 years old, a farm laborer); Jeremiah Mason (12 years old, a farm laborer) and Robert Mason (10 years old, a farm laborer). There is also a stepson, Israel Nelson, (29 years old, a farm laborer).[43] The ages of the family subtracted from the census year (1880) give approximate dates of birth as follows:

- Jeremiah Mason 1813/14
- Eliza Mason (wife) 1823/24
- Eliza Mason (daughter) 1863/64
- Charles Mason 1865/66
- Jeremiah Mason 1867/68
- Robert Mason 1869/70
- Israel Nelson 1850/51

The census also tells us that the father was born in South Carolina, the mother was born in Virginia, and all the children were born in Tennessee. No one in the family (either parents or children) can read or write.[44]

The similarities between these two entries are striking. Mother Eliza's name and place of birth in Virginia is the same. The names and ages of most children correspond. Young Eliza's date of birth is identical to that of Elsy's (whose name, of course, may be an affectionate diminutive of Eliza). Robert's name and date of birth in the 1880 return are consistent with the 1870 return. Young Jerry's name, of course, is possibly a diminutive of Jeremiah. Israel Mason/Israel Nelson have similar forenames and dates of birth. We will discuss the relationship of Israel to the family later.

But of course there are also pronounced differences between the two families. The first is the difference in the name of the father, "Cherry" versus "Jeremiah." Cherry's place of birth is given as Virginia in the first census, and Jeremiah's place of birth is given as South Carolina in the later one. The husband's date of birth varies in both (1824 versus 1814), as does his wife's (1826/1827 versus 1823/24). Children Joe Mason and Mary Mason are missing from the second return.

The birth dates of some children are also off. Charley is reported as 5 years old in 1870. If this is our Charles Harrison Mason, and he was born in September as the accepted family tradition suggests and his death certificate affirms, this can mean several things:

- He was 5 in June 1870, having had his last birthday in September 1869 (meaning he was born in September 1864)
- He was 4 years old in June 1870, soon to turn 5 in September 1870 and his father rounded up to the closest birthday, less than three months away. This would mean he was born in September 1865.
- He was 3 years old in June 1870, soon to turn 4 in September 1870 (which is consistent with the September 1866 birthdate claimed by his daughter) but the informant miscalculated, forgot or misspoke.

A similar dynamic applies in the 1880 census. If Charles was 14 in 1880, he either had his 14th birthday the previous September (meaning he was born in 1865), or he was 13 and soon to have his 14th birthday and the family rounded up (meaning he was born in 1866).

There is a similar difficulty in determining the birth date of the son, Jerry Mason. He was 4 years old in the 1870 census, but we don't know the month or day of his birth. If he was born early in the year (say March), he would have had his fourth birthday already, meaning he was born in 1866. If he was born later in the year (say November), his birthday was still to come (meaning he would have been turning five), which suggests a birth date of 1865. A similar kind of analysis applies to Jeremiah Jr.'s dates in the 1880 census. A 12-year-old Jeremiah either already had his 12th birthday (meaning he was born in 1868) or was to turn 13 later that year (giving a date of birth in late 1867).

WEIGHING THE EVIDENCE

So when was Charles Harrison Mason born? September 1856? September 1864? September 1865? September 1866? Was father Jerry born in 1814 (as the 1880 return says)? 1824 (as the 1870 return attests)? 1830 (as the marriage record of the Freedmen's Bureau would have us believe)? Was he born in Virginia or South Carolina? Or neither? Are these two discrete and separate families? The difficulty of resolving that mystery cannot be understated, given the dearth of records that survive for Black sharecroppers of the period.

Here is what we can accept as probable: "Cherry" is a clear variant on "Jerry." Class differences, regional dialects, and different levels of education lead to differences in enunciation, pronunciation, and spelling. It was to overcome just such problems as these that Soundex was developed in the late nineteenth century, to index phonetically equivalent names (e.g., Coen, Cohen, Cone, Conn, etc.). Such differences are also possible, even likely, for some forenames (e.g., Jan, John, Jon, etc.). Jerry, or some other member of the family, could have provided his name in a Southern drawl, and the census taker wrote down what he heard. No one would have clarified matters by spelling Jerry's name, as he and other family members were illiterate.

Mishearing may also account for Jerry's excessive age. He may have said 56 and the census taker heard 66. Or, more likely, since the family was illiterate, he may have given some sort of reference to when he was born and the census taker miscalculated. Since both censuses make clear we are dealing with an uneducated family, it is likely no one learned to compute dates and ages; subsequently, the parents' dates of birth, as well as their children's (and subsequently everyone's age) would always have to be approximate (e.g., Father: "I think Young Jerry was born in the year of the freak snow storm." Census Taker: "So he would be about 4"). As noted by Jerry Mason's contemporary Frederick Douglass:

> *Genealogical trees did not flourish among slaves. A person of some consequence in civilized society, sometimes designated as father, was literally unknown to slave law and to slave practice. I never met a slave in that part of the country who could tell me with any certainty how old he was. Few at that time knew anything of the months of the year or of the days of the month. They measured the ages of their children by spring-time, winter-time, harvest-time, planting-time, and the like. Masters allowed no questions concerning their ages to be put to them by slaves. Such questions were regarded by the masters as evidence of an impudent curiosity.*[45]

What then of more substantive differences (e.g., the difference in name between censuses)? If he was born "Jerry," why is the 1880 head of household identified as "Jeremiah"? Does the difference in name and difference in state of origin indicate this is a different individual (and, hence, this is not C.H. Mason's family)? To answer the name question, we must keep in mind that names frequently were changed after war, often as slaves' first act of freedom. Many slaves had no surnames until after the war. For example, Booker T. Washington in his autobiography recounts:

When they were slaves, a coloured person was simply called "John" or "Susan." There was seldom occasion for more than the use of the one name. If "John" or "Susan" belonged to a white man by the name of "Hatcher," sometimes he was called "John Hatcher," or as often "Hatcher's John." But there was a feeling that "John Hatcher" or "Hatcher's John" was not the proper title by which to denote a freeman; and so in many cases "John Hatcher" was changed to "John S. Lincoln" or "John S. Sherman," the initial "S" standing for no name, it being simply a part of what the coloured man proudly called his "entitles."[46]

Or, as expressed more succinctly by African American genealogist Ruth Randall, one of the "unique brick walls and barriers" encountered by researchers is "the tendency of former slaves to change surnames one or more times before settling on a permanent surname."[47]

No doubt this applied to forenames as well as surnames. It needs to be noted that slave names were frequently nicknames or infantilized forms of names (e.g., "Kitty," "Lizzy," "Billy," etc.). Again, this should not be a surprise. Those of a certain age will remember not so long ago even adult Black males were derisively addressed as "boy." In moving from Tennessee (the last place he was likely enslaved before service in the Union army) to Arkansas (where he could exercise some of the freedom won by the war), Jerry likely would have used the opportunity to claim an adult variation on his name ("Jeremiah"), rather than the child's name he was given ("Jerry").

Or it may have been an effort on Jerry's part to assert his dignity before the census taker, as later evidence clearly asserts that a Jerry (identified as such) and Eliza Mason lived in Plumerville, Arkansas. The 1887 List of Personal Property in Plumerville (Howard County), Arkansas indicates that Jerry Mason, Colored, was liable to pay a poll tax. He resided in School District 39, and the value of all his personal property (i.e., house, land, animals, wagons, etc.) totaled $4,000.[48] Similar entries appear for 1889 (for Mrs. E. Mason) and 1893 (for Eliza Mason).[49] The presence in the tax registers of cattle, hogs, carriages, and other entries suggests this was a settled family and they had been so for some time.

As to the discrepancy in the place of birth for Jerry Senior, to determine his actual place of birth is beyond the scope of this paper and would require its own investigation. Unlike the 1940 census, we have no way of knowing who actually provided the census information for the 1880 census. Was it someone who should have known, or someone who was guessing? Was it Jerry? Eliza? One of the older children? At this distance, we just don't know. Still, it is curious that if Jerry Mason was born in South Carolina, and Charles Harrison Mason knew that, no other census record ever mentions that fact. We have seen what the 1870 and 1880 censuses have to say about Mason and his father. The 1890 census no longer exists, and C.H. Mason cannot be located definitively in the 1900 census. With Mason clearly ensconced in Memphis after 1900, locating him in later returns becomes easier: the 1910 census stipulates that his parents were both born in Tennessee;[50] The 1920 census mentions Charles' parents were born in Virginia and Tennessee;[51] while the 1930 census indicates they were both born in Tennessee.[52] The 1940 census did not ask questions concerning the birth place of parents. In short, the states associated with Mason's parents are clearly the ones commonly associated with the family in the nineteenth century returns: Tennessee and Virginia. No mention of South Carolina is to be found anywhere. The confused response to such a simple question is explainable. A careful review of the census records suggests Charles Mason himself never responded to census takers questions. He frequently was absent the day the census taker arrived, and someone else had to provide the information, someone less knowledgeable than he. Clearly either his family did not know Jerry was from South Carolina, or he was definitely born elsewhere. The available evidence suggests the latter.

Consistency in the name and place of birth of the wife, similarity in the names of the children, consistency in dates of birth for most of them and places of birth for them all (except the father) suggests strongly that the census records cited here for 1870 and 1880 are for the same family. Moreover, the family is where it should have been according to the oral tradition maintained by the family, with the exception of Joe and Mary who, given their ages in the 1870 census, likely were grown and had left to establish their own families.

WHEN WAS CHARLES HARRISON MASON BORN?

What this means for the central question before us is this: it is certain that Charles Harrison Mason was not born in the late 1850s or early 1860s. As the oldest surviving document testifying to his origins, it is likely that the 1870 U.S. census is the more trustworthy source we have for his date of birth. Given the age listed in that census, it is more probable that Charles Harrison Mason was born in September 1864 than any other date. We can also affirm that Jerry Mason was Charles Harrison Mason's father and that he did not die at Fort Pillow or at any time when Charles was a very small child. When exactly Jerry did die is beyond the scope of this paper, but the difference in entries between the 1887 List of Persons and Personal Property Assessed for Taxation in Howard County, Arkansas (when Jerry Mason is listed), and the 1889 List (when Mrs. E. Mason is listed)[53] implies a date of death around 1888. Given the discrepancy in ages between the Freedmen's Bureau marriage record and the 1870 census, we can only say that Mason's father was born between 1824 and 1830, while Eliza was born a few years later. The most likely state in which to start looking for surviving slave records related to the parents' births (if such exist) would be Virginia (not South Carolina).

We can also consider it probable that Jerry's master relocated from Virginia to Tennessee, as the 1870 and 1880 census records attest all of his children were born in the latter state, even for those children born before his military service and wedding ceremony. We don't know when Jerry and Eliza met, but, contrary to the Freedmen's Bureau record, it was more than three years before the ceremony (i.e., before 1862); the elder children's ages suggest that. Also, it is clear that Jerry's wife Eliza *did have* other children before her marriage to Jerry. Israel Nelson is clearly labeled a stepson according to the 1880 census. Eliza's will indicates the names of her surviving children, and she stipulates she has two Nelson children: Israel Nelson and Joe Nelson.[54] So, the Joe Mason mentioned in the 1870 census should be understood to be Joe Nelson. That being so, based on the Freedmen's Bureau marriage record, we can assert that Jerry and Eliza had children before slave marriages were legally recognized. It is likely those children were Mary Mason (b. 1857?), Elsy (young Eliza) Mason (b. 1863?) and Charles Harrison Mason himself (born, most likely, in September 1864).

In relation to the Nelson siblings, it is not clear at this writing who Israel and Joe's father was, but it should be understood that they were Charles Harrison Mason's half-brothers, Eliza's sons by another father.[55] Israel was a Black preacher. At the time of C.H. Mason's conversion, he was baptized, ordained, and licensed to preach by Israel Nelson in the Black Baptist church in Plumerville.[56] So it is to Israel Nelson that the credit should go in starting Mason on the preaching career that resulted in the major church body we know today as the Church of God in Christ, with headquarters in Memphis, Tennessee.

3

African Roots and Multicultural Mission of Afropentecostalism

Bishop Mason's Desk of Roots[1]

Craig Scandrett-Leatherman

Bishop Charles H. Mason prayed that "God would give him a religion like that he heard the old folks talk about and manifest in their lives."[2] These "old folks" were Mason's elders and ancestors, ex-slaves who talked about and demonstrated a power that ended slavery and brought the slaves through it. The processes of enslavement and the middle passage, combined with the destruction of African languages and the African cultural heterogeneity, might have led to the destruction of African culture among African descendants in the United States, but it did not. Instead, Afropentecostalism as initiated by William J. Seymour, and the Church of God in Christ (COGIC) as developed by Charles Mason, conjoined African spirituality and Christian holiness theology. By connecting African views and ways of participating in a moral universe with holiness teachings and biblical visions of a just God, gracious Jesus, and generous Holy Spirit, these diverse cultural experiences-expressions were wed and embodied as joyous worship and social ethics. This joining empower(ed) participants to face challenges.

Contemporary COGIC rituals draw from African cultural soil, where rhythm and drum facilitate physical and social healing as a tradition that can be identified through an African healing institution. *Ngoma* is an African-derived drum ritual that is not only a playful pastime but a central institution that connects participants to the Spirit–to God's moral universe–and thereby empowers them to overcome or "go through" earthly hardships, social oppression, and sickness, and to experience–even while going through–the spiritual abundance of joy, dignity, and healing. This ritual work is accomplished by destroying barriers and blockages that would otherwise hinder the flow of spirit and resources.

This essay will work backwards to the ancient African tradition of *ngoma* and forward to COGIC's contemporary mission. First, I will outline an argument of African diaspora theory, which allows an investigation of the African roots of U.S. Afropentecostalism. Second, eighteen characteristics will be noted that indicate significant correspondences of cultural practices between *ngoma* and the Church of God in Christ. Third, a brief analysis will be offered on how Charles Mason and the Saints revised both the form and meaning of two of these corresponding practices. In conclusion, this chapter outlines two missiological implications of this study.

I first observed the healing power of African ritual in a Chicago drug recovery program that became increasing effective when the program was connected to Afropentecostal churches. The effectiveness was observed in reduced recidivism of residents in the program. Later, after a three-week assignment in Africa, it seemed to me that Black Pentecostalism in Chicago was more "African" than the mission-initiated churches that I attended on African soil. This essay and my Church of God in Christ membership is part of a call and project to understand and describe the cultural components of my subjective sense of power and "Africanicity." The ancient healing institution of the African drum is presented as a cultural root that Bishop Charles Mason Christianized and contextualized. The argument that COGIC practice is rooted in an ancient ritual practice of healing is based primarily on cultural observations and a theory of African diaspora. My aim is to increase understanding of the cultural roots of Afropentecostalism, and thereby to contribute to a revitalization of Afropentecostal and COGIC mission. I begin by outlining an argument for the African roots of Afropentecostalism.

BLACK PENTECOSTALISM AND ANCIENT NGOMA HEALING PRACTICE

Based on his extensive experience with both New World and African cultures, anthropologist Melville Herskovits argued that African descendants in the United States demonstrated the most assimilation and the least cultural continuity of African communities in the New World.[3] Three factors led Herskovits to this conclusion. First was the relatively small and culturally mixed group of Africans who where "imported" into the United States.[4] Of the six to ten million slaves who were brought from Africa to the New World, only 5 percent of these came to the United States–95 percent were taken to the Caribbean and to Central and South America. Furthermore, the United States slaves represented the most diverse group of Africans (unlike some colonies that "imported" Africans from only one region). The small percentage of slaves, along with their mixed ancestry, meant that U.S. slaves had to use English to communicate with each other and with Euro-Americans. A second factor that would have promoted assimilation to colonial culture was small plantation size. The United States averaged 12 slaves per plantation; at the other end of the continuum was Brazil, which averaged 100 slaves per plantation. Together the factors of mixed languages and cultural groups, and small slave group size, meant that in the American diaspora of Africans, U.S. slaves would have had the greatest dependence on and the greatest contact with colonial culture. Third, the United States increased its slave holdings primarily by reproduction, rather than importation. Though the United States imported less than 5 percent of exported African slaves, by 1850 African Americans in the United States and Canada made up over 30 percent of African descendants in the New World.[5] This increased U.S. percentage of Blacks in America demonstrates the U.S. slaveholders' preference to reproduce rather than import additional slaves from Africa. These three factors–greater mix of African languages and cultures, closer contact with colonial culture, and the least amount of ongoing African contact because of fewest imports–help to explain Herskovits' observation that U.S. African Americans demonstrated the least *quantity* of "Africanisms" in the New World.

Nonetheless, Herskovits also observed a persistence and concentration of African cultural continuity in the religious practices of U.S. Blacks. The practices of dance, drum, syncopated rhythms, and call and response communication characterize these continuities. While African American Christianity does not display the direct religious transfer of African religions–as does Haitian vodou, Brazilian candomblé, or Cuban santería,[6]–African American Christianity, especially Afropentecostalism, does demonstrate significant roots in an ancient African religious institution that is the cultural basis of all these forms of African diaspora religion in the Americas.

The discernment of the African roots of Pentecostalism, like the discernment of African history itself, requires a revision of the historical methods that have privileged attention to kings, conquests, and concepts. African roots are best discerned by methods analogous to the historic-linguistic methods that identify linguistic family trees by recording and mapping concentrations, influences, and distributions. Such linguistic studies provide a foundation, for additional archeological and anthropological study, to discern cultural patterns, networks, and distributions in (African) history.

The distributions of words and practices hint at historic habits of the daily and mundane world of ancient Africans, and recent linguistic studies provide an empirical and historical basis of African signifying and syncretizing (an emphasis on incorporating new experiences, cultures, peoples, or technologies rather than rejecting or destroying them).[7] Historiographies based on (past) lived experience[8] are more likely to discern relationships with contemporary practices than traditional historical methods that focus on kings, conquests, and concepts. Since words arc associated with practices, they reveal internal political relations, but also region relationships, as shared words (and related practices) suggest relationships. Thus, Jan Vansina has advanced the political history of ancient Africa grounded in historical-linguistic studies of Bantu languages,[9] which use lexicostatistical studies (counting common words and mapping them geographically) of Yvonne Bastian, André Coupez, and Michael Mann.[10] Their work also led David Lee Schoenbrun to conclude that the distribution pattern of Bantu cognates (root words)[11] indicates that language innovations occur in multiple locations, so that the Bantu language family did not develop in a single cultural center and then spread by migration and conquest; rather, it was broadly developed through diffused interrelationality (shared trade, technology, ideas, rituals–and words).[12] Based on this style of linguist development, Vansina suggests that the metaphor used to describe Bantu language development and distribution should shift from that of roots (of origin) and branches (of conquest-migration) to that of "waves" in order to emphasize its diverse centers of influence and broadly syncretistic style.[13] Though recent linguistic revisions identify a syncretistic style that has influence in the United States (and throughout the African diaspora, but especially concentrated in music and religion), the principle remains that broader geographic distribution of Bantu words indicates their older origins. The word *bantu* itself is one of the most broadly distributed African words that mean "people."[14]

In addition to the syncretistic style of Bantu language development–which finds (re)expression in the diversity of musical instruments used in COGIC worship, and in the incorporation-innovation of COGIC's musical styles–a prevalent Bantu word(-practice) finds particular continuity in COGIC worship. John Janzen has highlighted the fact that one of the most common words used predominantly throughout the Bantu languages is the word *ngoma*, which can simply be translated as "drum." The word corresponds with a particular drum that is used in many African regions, but, more importantly, the word *refers to the drum-dance-healing tradition*. The word, drum-and dance-healing-institution continue to be prevalent throughout sub-Saharan Africa both in traditional religions and in African Independent Churches.[15] The institution of *ngoma* is widespread throughout central and southern Africa. Also, the widespread distribution of the word *ngoma* indicates its origins in early Bantu civilization several thousand years ago.[16] In a comparative study in Congo, Tanzania, Zimbabwe, and South Africa, Janzen examines contemporary distributions of the interrelated "words, acts, and things" that led to a discernment of adaptive meanings and practices of *ngoma's* ancient institution.[17] Since this institution was dispersed throughout the cultures from which U.S. slaves were drawn, Janzen suggests that the ngoma traditions could be expected to occur in religious practices of Africans in the diaspora. Could it be that the ancient institution of *ngoma* is a significant cultural root of slave religion and Mason's Christian innovation? Was his Black-interracial mission in the United States informed, in part, by African ritual syncretism that had been embodied, not only in his ancestors, but also in his being and habits?

Donald Dayton has claimed that, for a theological analysis of Pentecostalism, factors of culture and race "may largely be ignored,"[18] but if "roots" of practice are sought, then cultural forms of ritual and bodily performance must be examined; historical analysis can be enhanced as the anthropological focus on what people do is allowed to complement the theological emphasis on origin of ideas. Dayton, Amos Yong, and others have well outlined theological roots of Pentecostalism,[19] but if the African roots of Pentecostalism are to be considered, then cultural practice must continue to be studied.[20] The case could be made that the Afro-cultural influence was central to the development of Pentecostal practice at and beyond Azusa; here I argue that the Azusa Street Revival in Los Angeles provided a space for continuities of African practice which had not been afforded in other denominations–even holiness camp meetings. Human emotion and spiritual-bodily expression was more tolerated in holiness circles, but the experiential base of knowledge, and of being touched by the Holy Ghost, found its fullest joy and most bodily expression under William J. Seymour in Los Angeles in a building on Azusa Street–and under Charles H. Mason as he took the experience (and style) back to Mississippi, Arkansas, and Tennessee. Highlighting the ritual-culture roots of Afropentecostalism is not to minimize the spiritual or theological aspects but to accentuate its significance and often neglected African roots. Having suggested a source of COGIC worship in the African institution of *ngoma*,[21] I will now describe contemporary and transatlantic characteristics that substantiate a ngoma-origin hypothesis.

African Religious Forms in Church of God in Christ Practice

In a similar way that correspondences of linguistic cognates indicate common origins and language families, so cultural practices may be compared to suggest or deny common origins. I have identified eighteen practices that indicate significant continuity between African *ngoma* and Church of God in Christ practices, which suggests common origin. These features are not or are minimally shared by "White" Pentecostals, so their origin is not theological or European. A few of these features are shared with other African American Protestant traditions (but many of them were "preserved" or concentrated in Afropentecostalism and have re-emerged in other Black denominations in recent decades). The eighteen common features are: Corporate encounters with the Holy Spirit usually involve (1) drums and (2) dance; sometimes the (3) rituals extend into the night; (4) wealth/money is valued in its social flow and agency is expressed in that flow; (5) call and response communication; (6) gender roles are distinguished with a dual, parallel, and interdependent political structure; (7) financial tribute is given to the leader and redistributed by him; (8) health is both physical and social, and the restoration of health is enacted in corporate ritual;

(9) abundance is expressed and experienced socially in good relations where wealth flows; (10) chiefs or leaders who accumulate too much wealth and who redistribute too little are suspect and may be accused of witchcraft or embezzlement; (11) pilgrimage is annually undertaken to the home area of the chief leader; (12) cosmology–or belief systems and belief images–are communicated primarily through rituals (which produce physical expressions, cosmologies, and behavior) as well as through teaching; (13) men are given prominence to speak in many mixed-gender ritual settings; (14) elders speak first and have greater authority, deference, and honor; (15) the term "Mother" is used for women with elder political status, and these mothers usually have veto power and significant economic power; (16) music varies in tempo and in complexity of polyrhythms in correspondence with various spirits of expressions or characteristics of the Spirit; (17) ancestors are alive and active in the community; (18) roots and other symbol-medicines (*minkisi*) exhibit strong power to heal either medicinally and/or by astonishment and wonder.

While all of these African ritual-political practices are or were shared by the Church of God in Christ, by African Indigenous Churches (AICs), and by many other African religious systems in Africa and its diaspora, they are absent in Protestant White practice–even in White Pentecostalism. *Ngoma*, by its prevalence throughout sub-Saharan Africa and by the prevalence of parallels in religions of the African diaspora, seems to be a ritual-cultural foundation of Afropentecostalism in the United States, especially in the Church of God in Christ. We now examine how Charles Mason converted aspects of this African institution to discipline descendants of ex-slaves in the United States.

Mason's Biblical Contextualization of African Religious Practice: Roots and Dance

Of the eighteen practices that I have identified as common to *ngoma* and Afropentecostalism, two will be described here: plant roots because they provide a visual illustration; and, second, dance, because this practice demonstrates conscious contextualization by Bishop Charles Mason. In one of very few essays that he published, Mason recognized critiques of these African practices from both Black and White Christians, and intentionally addressed these critiques on biblical grounds. His essay provides a terse but profound theology of cultural syncretism (missiology). Before proceeding to his missiology, we examine his roots.

Pictures of roots are prominent in early Church of God in Christ histories. Mary Mason's book *The History and Life Work of Elder C. H. Mason, Chief Apostle and his Co-Laborers*, has one picture of Charles H. Mason alone, which shows him holding a handlike root; six other pictures of roots are printed in the first several pages of the book, while pictures of his co-laborers don't show up until page 100 of the 140-page book.[22] In another book, a photo used to announce "Founders Day, May 31, 1953" shows Bishop Charles Harrison Mason behind a desk with a dozen or so roots on the desk. He is holding the one that looks like a human hand, and another that is attached to or wrapped around a stick; another large root forms a 360 degree loop, another seems to have chains wrapped and looped around it.[23] In his history of Mason and the Church of God in Christ, Bishop Ithiel Clemmons indicates that Mason was criticized "for bringing 'magic' into the church," where his collections of crooked roots and misshapen potatoes were on display, but Clemmons recalls that Mason described the roots not as magic but as "mystical wonders of God."[24]

In Africa, *ngangas*,[25] healing doctors, often used minkisi (medicines of wonder; plural of *nkisi*), natural objects decorated with human products, to create wonder and astonishment; such objects of wonder helped to produce a space and a people ripe with readiness and expectation.[26] Further wonder was experienced and created by African healers when the ritual was accompanied by drum and music, and induced human participation such as trembles, jumps, shouts, and dance.[27] Robert Farris Thompson, Professor of African Art History at Yale University, writes:

> According to Congo mythology, the very first *nkisi* [medicine of wonder] given to man by God was Funza, distributor of all *minkisi* [medicines of wonder], himself incarnate in unusual twisted-root formations. So "when you see a twisted root within a charm," Fu-Kiau Bunseki comments, "you know, like a tornado hidden in an egg, that this *nkisi* is very, very strong–you cannot touch it; only *nganga* [a healing doctor] can touch it."[28]

An African background of Bishop Mason's roots is suggested by this literature on African roots and medicines of wonder (*nkisi*).

Certainly other African "root doctors" can be found among the slaves in the United States, and Mason might have rejected "root involvement," except that, in scripture, God often used natural objects (any or all of the created order) to create wonder and thereby communicate about God's character.[29]

While *ngoma* often involved objects of wonder and power (*minkisi*) to prepare people for the Holy Spirit, drumming rhythms and dance were always used in *ngoma* rituals as expressions of receptivity to and participation in the (S)pirit. D.J. Young may have reintroduced dance from slave religion into the Church of God in Christ,[30] but C.H. Mason defended it in an essay, "Is It Right for the Saints of God to Dance?" The first word of the essay answers the question of the title: "Yes."[31] He goes on, "The Word of the Lord says: 'let them praise him in the dance' Pss 149:3, also 150:4." The First half of the 400 word essay quotes 15 passages of scripture, which culminate in the Gospels with the teachings of Jesus–that angels dance when sinners repent, and that dancing marked the return of the prodigal son; the next fourth exegetes those passages, and the last fourth distinguishes the dance of the Saints from the dance of "the world." Bishop Mason ends with a benediction: "How sweet it is to dance in Him and about Him (Christ), for he that dances in the Spirit of the Lord expresses joy and victory. Amen."[32]

Contextualization is the task of making, selecting, and revising cultural practices to make them meaningful and useful in fulfilling Jesus' commission to make disciples of all nations.[33] Charles Mason's essay, taken with the practice of roots, reveals several principles for contextualizing a Christian ritual practice beyond the cultural forms through which it is introduced. The first principle is: if a cultural practice does not contradict biblical ethics, then it may be considered as a means to communicate Christ. This principle is or can be based on scriptures already cited, indicating that God made all and therefore can communicate through all. Rejection of so-called "magical" or strange cultural forms need not be made out of hand. One culture's "magic" may be another culture's "wonderment." Since Paul indicates that all things were created in, for, and toward Christ–in him all things hold together (Col. 1:16–17), then all things can be useful for communicating God's Good News. The second principle, however, is that the Bible is a basis of determining the appropriateness of using a cultural practice for communicating the Gospel. The flow of Mason's essay on dance might suggest that the practice and teaching of Jesus is the highest authority within scripture. Thus, Mason's exegesis is Christocentric; the center of his essay is Christ's teaching with the parable of the prodigal who was received with music and dancing. The third principle is an extension of the second. The cultural form must be able to glorify Christ and fulfill his commands. Mason uses Christ as the aim of the practice: "[D]ancing of the people of God is to be in the spirit of Jesus only, for as in Jesus only we rejoice and dance and praise God."[34] The question here is, can the ritual or cultural practice be used to glorify God, and for Mason the priority would be on praise. The fourth principle is that the cultural practice must be distinguished from the old form, which did not or does not give praise to God. "The people of God do not dance as the world dances." Saints dance "by the Spirit of God" and "to the glory of God" and "to satisfy the soul."[35]

Against "mainline" church tendencies (Baptist and Methodist) to practice the politics of respectability,[36] David Daniels, Walter Hollenweger, Leonard Lovett, Arthur Paris, Thomasina Neely, and James Tinney have all suggested that, through the medium of slave religion and holiness camp meetings,[37] Mason Africanized the Black church. Robert Franklin has suggested that through the incorporation of "drums, spontaneous song celebrations, call-and-response preaching, dancing, and emotionally liberating worship" Mason "sought to re-Africanize Black churches."[38] I have outlined Church of God in Christ practices that have African roots and correspondences and have summarized the principles by which Mason incorporated and revised those practices. It may be said of COGIC that its participants form the most popular Afrocentric institution in the United States, yet, in its own theology, it does not explicitly focus on African practice; instead it (implicitly) justifies its (African) practices based on the (Hebraic-Greek) Bible. The phenomenal growth of Pentecostalism in general and the Church of God in Christ in particular may demonstrate what Lamin Sanneh has called the translatability of Christianity–that it thrives by being rooted in cultures.[39] I would argue that Pentecostalism in particular allows or promotes this translatability. Being Christocentric can mean being Afrocentric. Though this essay has only briefly described two of many cultural practices that suggest African cultural roots of COGIC practices–roots on Mason's desk and dance in COGIC worship–these practices give evidence of an

African cultural root in addition to theological and holiness ritual roots.

Missiological Implications

Afropentecostalism's mission has two seemingly contradictory but actually complementary directions: Afrocentric and multicultural. Though we might have hoped that the problem of the twentieth century identified by Du Bois[40] as the color-line would have been obliterated, instead it persists. The continued over-representation of African Americans in prisons,[41] with lesser wealth[42] and lower-paying jobs, in substandard housing and schools, testifies, along with the rapping anger of Black youth, that racism is still rampant in our society. In such a setting the Church of God in Christ may again develop its tradition of using African or Afrocentric cultural forms to communicate the liberating news of Jesus Christ and the empowerment of the Holy Spirit. Cultural forms of communication such as rap–which has African roots–need to be incorporated in our mission and into at least some churches. The paradox of the Great Commission is that it must be rooted in particular cultures yet extended to other cultures at the same time;[43] this always begins with mission between the generations–each respecting and being stretched by the "culture" of the other generation–but it also extends across cultures (and races). In Acts 13:1 we see that, in the transition from Judaism to Christianity, the spiritual center had moved from Jerusalem to Antioch, and that the leaders of the Antioch movement were a multicultural group of prophets and teachers named Barnabas, Simeon who was called Niger, Lucius of Cyrene, Manaen who had been brought up with Herod the tetrarch, and Saul. Jesus' work on the cross had broken barriers and created a new society made up of a Roman official, a Jewish scholar, one or two people of African descent, a Greek, and priest.[44] This was the group that discipled Paul and sent him on his mission to the Gentiles. If there is any doubt that he was influenced by his experience with this group, Paul makes it clear that the social consequence of Jesus death and resurrection is the destruction of human barriers of class, race, and gender; he writes: "There is neither Jew nor Greek, there is neither slave nor free; there is neither male nor female, for you are all one in Christ Jesus" (Gal. 3:28, NKJV).

One danger of the Church of God in Christ is that by institutionally honoring its ancestors and elders it may lose sight of its mission to pass on its faith to the next generation as it clings too closely to the forms of its faith in previous generations. The example of music must suffice. Timothy Kalil points out that when COGIC moved its headquarters to Memphis it located near Beale Street, which was the city's center of Black popular music and, relatedly, Mattie Moss Clark reviews the expansion of musical instruments incorporated into COGIC worship.[45] Will the musical styles and instruments be similarly incorporated in COGIC churches for the next generation (in the form of rap)[46] or will "their" musical genre be relegated to the realm of secular or "devil's music" and excluded from intergenerational (cross-cultural) worship? Paul Oliver suggests that musicality was central to COGIC's vitality and growth: "[I]n this musically rich area the appeal of a church which encouraged playing instruments in church was considerable and the new denomination spread rapidly."[47] A large survey, funded by Pew and coordinated by the Interdenominational Theological Center (ITC) of Atlanta found that of 1863 churches (of six of the largest Black denominations), the majority of COGIC churches (and the highest denominational percentage among surveyed denominations, 54.4 percent) indicated that they would never include rap music in Sunday morning worship.[48] Though men made up 21.2 percent of the COGIC congregations surveyed a much smaller percentage of men were represented among new members–despite the fact that 18-to-35-year-olds made up more than a third of COGIC's congregants (34.2 percent).[49] Young men are the most likely audience to identify with the social analysis and musical styles of rap. Rejected COGIC rappers may find inspiration in the history of COGIC musical innovation[50] and in contemporary acceptance of rap in some churches,[51] and find comfort in the fact that Thomas Dorsey was also initially rejected by most churches.[52] It may be that COGIC's early innovation and acceptance of Gospel music has changed (with aging leadership and generational style intolerance) to a stifling of continued innovations (with rap).

CONCLUSION

The movement of mission is both home and away from home, both familiar and stretching–lest we box God into "our culture" and thereby make God into an idol (of ourselves). Afropentecostalism still has an Afrocentric mission, for there is much transformation to be accomplished in African American communities. But it must also be multicultural (and intergenerational), for God's abode in heaven and on earth is a house of prayer for *all* the peoples–anything of a lesser vision and aim leads to an exclusive sanctuary that is self-serving, rather than inclusive and missional. Africanicity in its language development, in its (*ngoma*) ritual syncretism and healing, and in historic COGIC musical innovations were means of incorporating people, styles, and technologies into a vital and signifying peoplehood–into sanctifying sainthood, and into a holiness ethics of social transformation. When such processes cease, the church's vitality ceases and a particular cultural expression is upheld as holy in itself–rather than seeing holiness as a means of mission. But the mission-empowering Holy Spirit longs to infuse churches with power, with nondefensive witnessing boldness, and with healing: for bodies, between peoples–and between generations.

Afropentecostalism is in a good position to minister to many in the Euro-American culture, which, in its "postmodern" age, seems to have exhausted its absolute dependence on the god of reason, has become fascinated with cultural diversity, and has assimilated numerous forms of African culture, especially musical forms. It is in a good position to need the energy, vision, and styles of youth. At least part of the mission of Black Pentecostalism is to accentuate African roots and oppose the American consumerism that procured slaves and persists in racism and international injustice. The prosperity gospel that spiritualizes our nation's extraordinary consumption must be resisted even as Pentecostal experience and discipleship promote a richer prosperity oriented by holiness, sustained by thanksgiving for adequate abundance, and aimed at mission. In this mission, accentuating African roots is one means to celebrate the abundance of the Spirit in which the flow of feet, goods, possessions, food, praise, and salvation is manifested (Acts 2:43f) in the multicultural and unified body of Christ (Gal. 3:28; Acts 13:1) through which healing power flows and joyful worship abounds.

4

Charles Harrison Mason as Sign Reader and Interpreter

Frederick L. Ware

Charles Harrison Mason, founder of the largest Pentecostal denomination in the United States, the Church of God in Christ, taught and preached using signs (Figure 1).[1] A sign is "that by which anything is made known or represented."[2] Signs are observable objects and events whose meanings are not limited solely to their obvious appearance. They point to something or someone else. When a person looks at them, he or she sees more than the objects or events themselves. The sign, in whatever substance it happens to take shape, is not sacred. The significance of the object or event lies in its capacity to represent something of a spiritual nature. A sign becomes a symbol when it participates in (or is a part of) the reality to which it points.[3]

Mason taught and preached using animal life, trees, roots, vegetables, fruits, and events in nature as signs of God's glory, character, word, and will; profound spiritual truths; the imminence of the Second Coming of Jesus Christ; and the nearness of the end of the world. Mason used nature and agricultural illustrations that people who were tied to the land could understand and thereby grasp the transformative message of Holiness-Pentecostalism. None of the objects used or events cited by Mason achieved the status of symbols, based on the Tillichian notion of religious symbols. None of the signs were taken literally or regarded as identical (one and the same) with the Holy or anything in the spiritual realm. The objects were not idols, in the sense that persons worshiped them. Also, these objects were not instruments for worship.

REACTIONS TO MASON'S TEACHING AND PREACHING

Reactions to Mason's teaching and preaching were both positive and negative. C.G. Brown of Kansas City, Missouri, served as the first executive secretary of the Home and Foreign Mission Department of the Church of God in Christ. Brown recorded his observations of Mason's life, mannerisms, and style of worship and preaching, as well as the content verbatim of some of Mason's prayers and sermons.[4] For the most part, Brown believed that Mason possessed supernatural qualities. He was impressed with Mason's use of signs drawn from nature. He notes that all persons listening to Mason were fascinated with these material illustrations; the objects used by Mason were a sure way of getting persons' attention. Beyond Mason's ability to hold his audiences spellbound, Brown identifies four other effects of the signs: they (1) make known some mystery of God, (2) serve as warnings of God's wrath on sinfulness, (3) indicate that God has pronounced sentence on wicked persons, and (4), most importantly, enable persons to better understand God.

Brown's observations suggest that, in addition to Mason's moral integrity and charismatic spirituality, his use of signs was crucial to his effectiveness as a preacher. However, this use of signs must be understood not only on the individual level (i.e., Mason's creativity in constructing and using signs) but also on the group level (i.e., his audiences' recognition and acceptance of signs).[5] Mason, the sign-making and sign-reading preacher, exhibits the values, beliefs, and art of the culture that he shares with his audiences. Mason was reputed to have "the original rhythm of colored peoples."[6]

Whereas Brown uses the phrases "earthly signs" and "God's handiwork in nature" and shows some understanding of the homiletic and theological value of the objects, other persons observing Mason used the phrase "freaks of nature," a phrase with very negative connotations, in their discussion of the objects. The term "freak" conveys the notion that something is unusual or abnormal in the worst sense of the word.

Contrasting Brown's positive assessment of Mason's preaching is a negative report of Mason's Pentecostal meetings in the *Commercial Appeal*, which, at the time, was a principal newspaper in Memphis, Tennessee. The newspaper article follows the caption: "Versatile Negro Preacher Uses Freak Vegetables to Paint a Moral and Illustrate the Powers of God."[7] The reporter finds Mason's use of oddly shaped vegetables for sermon illustrations to be a "strange turn" in Negro religion. He describes Mason's interpretations of several sweet potatoes, an Irish potato, and an okra pod. According to the reporter, in Mason's collection, there were sweet potatoes said, in shape, to resemble a rattlesnake, seagull, parrot, turkey, duck, and a human heart. The Irish potato resembled a hen. The okra pod had grown in a circular pattern resembling a coiled snake. Mason used the sweet potato shaped like a heart to tell his listeners about having purity of heart–that is, the necessity of living righteously. The reporter admits not hearing Mason render any interpretation of the snake-shaped objects, but assumes that these objects were used in Mason's sermons about hell fire.[8] The reporter concludes that Mason's collection of objects is more suitable for display in a "dime museum" than in a church service.[9] He regards Mason's use of earthly signs as the most recent twist in an already bizarre Negro religion that interprets unusual weather as a sign of the end of the world and nearly any celestial event as a sign of imminent trouble.

Mason may have used these kinds of objects for sermon illustrations before his involvement in the Pentecostal movement. Mason was residing in Memphis well before he ever conducted Pentecostal meetings.[10] In 1862, thousands of newly emancipated slaves flocked to Memphis, a Union territory (Fort Pickering) that would not regain its charter as a city until 1893. After 1897, Mason was pastoring a small church in a south Memphis neighborhood. He did not attract a great deal of public attention in Memphis, the city where he would eventually choose to headquarter his Pentecostal organization, until his propagation of Pentecostalism. The brand of Pentecostalism that Mason learned was from the movement's founder, William J. Seymour, whose religious services were a mixture of Holiness and Pentecostal teachings, revivalism, and Black folk religion.[11] Seymour's meetings, like Mason's, were viewed negatively by the White press.[12] The enthusiasm of Pentecostal worshipers is described as being hysterical and irrational. In spite of the racial and religious bigotry of the White press, thousands of persons–Blacks, Whites, and other ethnic groups–flocked to these Pentecostal meetings.

Mason's Roots in the American South

At the turn of the twentieth century, in the year 1901, before the tides of industrialization and urbanization swept completely across the United States, nearly 40 percent of the total American population lived in cities and the remaining 60 percent, the majority of the population, still lived in rural areas.[13] With regard to the African American population, nine out of ten persons lived in the South, and more than 80 percent of these persons in the South lived in rural areas.[14] One hundred years later, based on the Year 2000 United States Census, 80.3 percent of the total American population lived in metropolitan areas.[15] Close to 90 percent of the African American population lived in these metropolitan areas.[16] The South continues to be the region of the United States that has the highest concentration of the Black population; 55.3 percent of African Americans live in the South.[17] To be more concise and to the point, at the turn of the twentieth century, the United States and especially its African American population was rural. The shift of residency from rural to urban areas did not result in an immediate disappearance of rural lifestyles. At the beginning of this movement of urbanization, cities in the South had a rural character to them. It was common then for persons living in cities to cultivate vegetable gardens and "[keep] chickens, horses, cows, hogs, and other animals."[18]

Though Mason traveled to various states within the continental United States and countries overseas, he was a southerner by birth and lived most of his life in the American South. He was born to Jerry and Eliza Mason, former slaves, on September 8, 1864, on the Prior Farm in Shelby County, Tennessee, in an area that today is near the town of Bartlett.[19] In 1878, a yellow fever epidemic forced the Mason family to move from Shelby County, Tennessee, to Plumerville, Arkansas.[20] Before Mason achieved notoriety as a minister, his principal work and livelihood was through sharecropping. From childhood unto early adulthood, he tended livestock and worked the fields–planting, cultivating, and harvesting crops.[21]

The start and early flourishing of Mason's ministry was in the South.[22] In 1891, he was licensed and ordained in Preston, Arkansas. By the year 1893, he came under the influence of the Holiness movement. In 1895, Mason meet Charles Price Jones in Jackson, Mississippi, and, from 1896 to 1899, the two men conducted Holiness conventions, revivals, and published several pamphlets. Their activities centered mostly in the south central states (i.e., Tennessee, Arkansas, Mississippi, and Louisiana) of the lower Mississippi River Valley between Memphis and New Orleans.

In 1897, after expulsion from the General Association of Baptist Churches, an unincorporated fellowship of Black Baptist churches, for overzealously propagating Holiness teachings; C.P. Jones and C.H. Mason, along with W.S. Pleasant and J.A. Jeter, organized a new group under the name "Church of God." Many congregations that were formed as a result of the Holiness movement named themselves "Church of God." In order for the group led by C.P. Jones and C.H. Mason to distinguish itself from other Church of God organizations, the name "Church of God in Christ" was used. Mason claimed that the name "Church of God in Christ" had been revealed to him and was confirmed in his reading of the New Testament, for example, in 1 Thessalonians 2:14. The new church unanimously accepted the name proposed by Mason. Their first permanent place of meeting was a cotton-gin house in Lexington, Mississippi. C.P. Jones was elected as general overseer of the new organization. C.H. Mason was appointed overseer of operations in Tennessee, J.A. Jeter overseer of operations in Arkansas, and W.S. Pleasant overseer of operations in Mississippi.

After Mason's Pentecostal experience in 1907 at the Azusa Street Revival, he parted from Jones on the issue of baptism in the Holy Spirit as a third work of grace that follows conversion and sanctification and tongue-speaking (glossolalia) as initial evidence of a believer's having had this spiritual baptism.[23] Those ministers who agreed with Mason met with him in Memphis, in September 1907, in order to reorganize the Church of God in Christ. At this meeting, the ministers retained the name "Church of God in Christ" for their organization and elected Mason as their leader, a position he held until his death on November 17, 1961.[24] The group of ministers led by Jones continued to the use the name "Church of God in Christ" for their organization but later, in 1915, changed the name of their organization to "Church of Christ (Holiness) U.S.A."

Headquartered in Memphis, the Church of God in Christ experienced tremendous growth under Mason's leadership. The church, which was once concentrated in the south central states along the lower Mississippi River Valley, spread as its members migrated from the South to the North, Midwest, Southwest, and West of the United States and traveled overseas. Mason actively expanded the Church of God in Christ's scope of mission into new territories while continuing to reside in Memphis, where Church of God in Christ members would gather annually at its Holy Convocation.

THE SOUTHERN CONTEXT DURING THE RISE OF PENTECOSTALISM

Following the Civil War, the South suffered a great agricultural crisis. Soil exhaustion and erosion resulted from the widespread development of staple crops (i.e., tobacco, sugar, rice, and cotton) in the South.[25] The problem of soil erosion was further complicated by the invasion of the boll weevil, pests that infested the south central and southeastern states.[26] The cotton industry, the major crop in the South, shifted westward to areas that had escaped infestation by the boll weevil.[27] The agricultural malady of the South was further complicated by natural disasters, particularly severe summer thunderstorms.[28]

While all persons in the South were affected by this agricultural crisis, African American suffering was extreme. All federal government efforts at land reform for the benefit of former slaves failed.[29] African Americans who wanted to escape the plantation system needed land and farms of their own. Some were able to purchase land, but the vast majority were sharecroppers, a status not far removed from their previous condition of slavery. "Well over 80 percent of black Americans lived on farms in the rural South in the late nineteenth century, and sharecropping touched their social, political, and economic lives."[30] Mechanization drove down the price of labor and even left many sharecroppers unemployed. Black farmers needed credit in order to buy food, clothing, machinery, seeds, supplies, and other necessities. Credit costs were high. With the problems of soil erosion, boll weevil infestation, and the demise of the cotton industry, black farmers fell deeper in debt. Rural blacks were close to the land and suffered immensely during the South's agricultural crisis. As resources became scarcer, African Americans were excluded from the economic mainstream, became victims of White lynch mobs, and relegated to second-class status through segregation laws.

It was during the South's agricultural crisis when Pentecostalism arose. Pentecostalism appealed to the disinherited, poor, and disillusioned in the South. After the Civil War, in the South and even in the North, poor Whites and Blacks were mobile, in a condition of rootlessness. These poor and disillusioned persons were searching for meaning. Pentecostalism supplied them with meaning, purpose, and answers.

Pentecostalism's Arminian conception of faith was empowering to persons beset with hopelessness. Pentecostal evangelists stressed that Jesus did not die only for a select few, but for all persons. They preached, "There's power in the blood and you can have this power! God's offer of salvation is for everyone. The power of Christ's atonement is available to all persons. By faith, exercising faith, or putting faith in Jesus Christ, a person can affect his or her own situation. The individual is not helpless against sin, evil, sickness, poverty, or racism. He can act, through faith in Christ and with the power that Christ gives, to change his condition." For persons economically depressed and politically disenfranchised, the spiritual disciplines and catharsis of Pentecostalism provided alternative methods of achieving social goods and maintaining sanity.[31] Pentecostals' optimistic perspective and theological justification of self-reliance appealed to persons who had come to realize that they could not depend on government or other social agencies. Pentecostalism empowered and motivated them to achievement through religion and spirituality.

BLACK FOLK BELIEFS ABOUT SIGNS

Newbell Niles Puckett's *Folk Beliefs of the Southern Negro* contains an extensive description of signs in Black folk culture. He identifies two principal types of signs: (1) control signs and (2) prophetic signs (or omens). Both types of signs are calls to and guides for action.[32] Puckett concludes, at the time of his having conducted this study, that signs are the largest body of spiritual beliefs among African Americans in the South.[33]

Both types of signs presuppose beliefs about causal relationships, according to Puckett.[34] Signs are referred to pejoratively as "superstitions" because these supposed causal relationships, for the most part, are disproved and shown to be false by modern science. For African Americans, with little or no access to formal education, the system of signs was necessary to overcome helplessness in the face of hostile forces and establish a framework for prudent and moral behavior.[35] Puckett says: "Bits of occupational-lore were handed down to the Negro agriculturalists (male and female) as a real part of farm training. To the early slaveholders, and especially to the ignorant overseers, the lore connected with agriculture was almost as important as the farming methods themselves; they were deemed so essential to self-maintenance that both lore and methods were handed down alike in the training of field hands, while other folk-beliefs were not considered so important."[36] Based on what Puckett is saying, as a matter of course and routine, African Americans working in agriculture were exposed to beliefs in signs. Learning signs was as important as learning the tasks of manual labor in farming.

Control signs are causal relationships about which humans can do something. The control signs are said to be positive when, if they are read properly, good results are achieved. The control signs are negative when bad results follow from some action persons either have taken or failed to have taken. The formula for these types of signs is: "If you (or someone else) behave in such and such a manner, so and so will happen."[37]

Prophetic signs are causal relationships about which humans can do nothing or those causal relationships created by chance, God, the devil, or spirits. Prophetic signs are called omens when the causal relationship is the cause of or precedes a future event. The formula for these types of signs is: "If something (outside of your control) behaves in such and such a manner, so and so will result."[38] While humans do not create the causal relationship, they can counteract most omens by exercise of proper conduct.

BLACK FOLK BELIEF AND AFRICAN TRADITIONAL RELIGIONS

Though Black southern folk culture may be a syncretism of European, American Indian, and African beliefs and practices, numerous studies focus on the influence of African traditional religions in the development of Black culture in the United States.[39] Lawrence W. Levine's *Black Culture and Black Consciousness* is not only one of the pioneering works in this pattern of scholarship but also a significant study of signs in Black folk culture. Levine claims that the ethos prevailing in the African culture from which the slaves came was reflected in the belief that life was not random or accidental. Levine states that African slaves believed that "[h]uman beings could 'read' the phenomena surrounding and affecting them because Man was part of, not alien to, the Natural Order of things... Survival and happiness and health depended upon being able to read the signs that existed everywhere, to understand the visions that recurrently visited one, to commune with the spirits that filled the world."[40] Levine adds that, in African American slave culture, "[Nature] provided signs that correctly read could help one to avoid, or at the very least, be prepared for a host of calamities and disasters. The universe was not silent; it spoke to those who knew how to listen ... There were signs indicating what the weather would be; signs telling of the coming of strangers or loved ones; signs prophesying bad luck or good fortune; signs warning of an impending whipping or the approach of White patrols; signs foretelling imminent illness or death."[41] Signs were common in African American life. As late as 1968, John Mason Brewer, premier African American folklorist, claimed that belief in signs was yet common in African American culture.[42]

There are five themes in African religions that are analogous to Southern folk belief about signs. They are: (1) the natural world is a "religious universe," imbued with meanings, (2) there are various objects and events that convey these religious meanings, (3) certain persons are skilled in identifying these religious objects and discerning God's word and will conveyed by them, (4) signs are an indication that God is active and participating in nature and human life, and (5) God judges human beings according to their regard or disregard for the truth conveyed by signs.

The first theme suggests that religious or spiritual meanings permeate the universe. We do not live in a cosmic machine whose existence is the result of random chance and which operates by strict laws unfriendly to human life. The belief in a religious universe is an affirmation that life is meaningful and purposeful.

Belief in religious objects follows from belief in a religious universe. Natural objects and events symbolize God's being and presence. African peoples "read" God into various phenomena that may be categorized as either heavenly (such as sun, moon, stars, rain, thunder, and wind) or earthly (such as earthquakes, floods, colors, numbers, and sounds).[43] The objects are not worshiped but rather the spirit or truth that they represent is reverenced.[44]

Belief in religious objects supports belief in and the function of religious specialists such as seers or diviners.[45] The diviners' main function is to find out hidden secrets (or knowledge) and pass these secrets (or it) on to other people. They discover hidden secrets through pebbles, nuts, shells, numbers, water, animal entrails, the palms of persons, dice, and any other objects that they consider significant for religious purposes.[46] They "see" things in these objects that are not easily detected by other people who are nonspecialists.

Their goal is to find the source of wrong or evil and what should be done to correct or eliminate it.

Most African peoples believe that wrong or evil arises because humans break the harmony of the cosmos and thus enter into conflict with a deity who acts as Judge.[47] God, they believe, is the final guardian of law and of the moral and ethical codes, and the one who punishes in this life. African peoples associate God with concepts of justice, punishment, and retribution. As Agent in human history, God visits the earth from time to time to inspect it, bestow blessings, and mete out punishment. God makes God's response felt through natural events and objects.

Folk belief in signs was foundational to the African American slave community. African American slaves apparently did not experience any cognitive dissonance between their folk beliefs and Christian beliefs. For many slaves, there were few tensions in the components of their religion. The components complemented and reinforced each other. They often used the Bible to prove the efficacy of their folk beliefs, and used their folk beliefs to validate Christian beliefs.[48] For example, in the experience of conversion and the call to preach, persons often asked for and sought signs to confirm whether their experience was genuine.[49] A biblical text such as Matthew 14:26, in which the disciples mistake Jesus for a spirit, could be taken as proof of the existence of ghosts, or another text, such as Exodus 7:8–13, in which the magicians of Pharaoh contest the wonders performed by Moses and Aaron, could be taken as proof of magic.[50]

Southern people conditioned their daily living around signs. Mason knew or intuited this and developed a preaching style that drove home the Pentecostal message to people coming from rural environments. He used Southern folk belief in signs to exhort persons to righteous living and to warn them of God's impending wrath and the imminent return of Christ. He may have been perceived by his listeners as a seer of hidden things and wise to the source of evil or trouble and what to do about it.[51] Mason's personal testimony is evidence of the influence of the religion of African American slaves upon him. He was born to slave parents and stated that when he was a child he would join his mother for devotions, "praying that God would give to him a religion like he heard the old folks talk about and manifested in their lives."[52]

Signs in Pentecostal Theology

J. Rodman Williams, a leading Pentecostal theologian, deals with signs primarily from the perspective of eschatology. Signs are evidence that indicate that Christ's return is near, according to Williams' interpretation of Pentecostalism. Based on Williams' study, signs indicating the imminence of Christ's return are: (1) the outpouring and remarkable manifestations of the Holy Spirit; (2) the spread of the Gospel to the whole world; (3) a worsening of the conditions of society; (4) religious apostasy; (5) the Anti-Christ; (6) exposure of the "Man of Sin"; (7) appearance of the two beasts mentioned in Revelation 13; (8) the Abomination of Desolation mentioned in the Book of Daniel; (9) the Great Tribulation, a period of persecution, affliction, and oppression; and (10) extraordinary phenomena in the heavens and on earth.[53] Within Williams' conceptual scheme, those signs upon which Mason, as a Pentecostal, focused are manifestations of the Holy Spirit, the spread of the gospel, an increase of evil in society, great tribulation, and unusual objects and events in the heavens and on the earth.

Mason had a definite biblical and theological conception of how signs function within the context of Christianity. Signs constitute a form of general revelation. Signs are public; they are for everyone to see. Mason understood signs to have four basic purposes. First, signs reveal God's wonder and mystery. According to Mason, God has a way, that is, through signs, to make humanity know that God is God. God reveals Godself in signs to believers. Ministers, out of all believers, are to inquire into the things of God, and explore the meaning of signs, according to Mason's reading of the Bible.[54]

Second, signs are instrumental in conversion, setting people free from sin and ignorance. Signs move people to conversion, to surrender to God. Mason claimed that God's children (i.e., believers) set humanity free through their interpreting of signs and performance of wonders.[55]

Third, signs are warnings. Mason believed that signs are confirmations of the imminent return of Christ and evidence of God's wrath. According to Mason, "[T]he day of the Lord [will] never come till the signs of the Lord appear."[56] He believed that the earth was producing those signs in order to let believers know that the end, the Day of the Lord, was near.[57]

Fourth, signs are calls to holiness. They reveal knowledge about appropriate moral and religious conduct. Signs can be read for guidance on how believers should live.

African American Pentecostals rarely acknowledge or affirm any connection of their beliefs and practices with beliefs and practices in Black folk culture, especially those beliefs and practices that are objectionable to their sensibilities as Pentecostals. Pentecostals perceive themselves as restorationists of the New Testament church. The Bible is their principal source of reference for explanations of their worship, beliefs, and practices. However, the message of Pentecost, as they have received it, did not come directly from the first century to the twentieth without mediation through history and various other sources. African Americans drew upon not only the Bible but also upon other sources, such as folk culture.

African American Christians remember Pentecost but do not remember the folk practices that are related empirically to their interpretation and practice of Pentecostalism. As with other persons of the same persuasion, Mason's principal identity is "Pentecostal," which influences how he appropriates and re-interprets folk belief. For Mason, the beliefs in signs are construed strictly for the service of propagating Pentecostalism. The perspective of Mason and other African American Pentecostals like him is compatible with H. Richard Niebuhr's typology of Christ and culture in paradox.[58] Pentecostals perceive culture and social institutions as part of a fading world order. The church represents an alternative to culture. Thus, there is little recognition of responsibility for shaping and guiding culture. African American Pentecostals perpetuate Black folk culture, but they do so unconsciously and uncritically, without evaluation of the credibility and functionality of these beliefs and practices. Though Pentecostals espouse and celebrate freedom, various cultural forms and conventional (or traditional) morality are observed and obeyed without question.

SIGNS IN MASON'S EXTANT SERMONS

Mason used a variety of signs to demonstrate God's wrath and the imminent return of Christ. On one occasion, he used severe thunderstorms in the south central states as a sign.[59] He stated that the storms resulted in the deaths of over 800 persons, injury to 3,000 persons, and property damage of about $15 million dollars.[60] He claimed that God was involved in the storms. He contended that

God directed the storms against lewdly dressed persons, shysters, corrupt judges, adulterers, oppressive employers, and aggressive nations.[61] Another sign of God's wrath and the imminent return of Christ is what Mason called "strange acts," bizarre, never before seen or heard of events and objects. For example, according to Mason, one such strange act was, during a storm, a team of mules being lifted by the wind and placed on top of a house.[62] Other strange acts during the storm were the wind's stripping a chicken of its feathers and a woman of her clothing. The nakedness of the woman and the unfeathered chicken were signs of God's exposing the sin of humankind.[63] Still other signs of God's wrath and Christ's return are disastrous phenomena. Mason stated: "Men are called in the earthquakes and storms, in fires, in lynchings, in burnings, in wars, and in distresses. He sent forth worms as armies to gather in the foodstuff. Nothing for a man to do, no labor for his hands to perform. God's hand is moving, giving men no time to pray."[64] Epidemics, such as the flu, are another form of disasters that are a sign of Christ's coming, according to Mason.[65]

The occurrence of disasters is not indicative of God's wrath only. The sparing of life during these disasters are signs of God's mercy. For example, during the season of great storms, Mason pointed to how a baby was taken up and carried away by the winds but landed without being hurt.[66] In another display of mercy, a mother and her twins were lifted by the winds and landed in a tree without being hurt.[67] These acts of divine mercy fall under Mason's concept of "strange acts."

In addition to disastrous events, Mason saw various objects in nature as signs. Mason spoke of: "Signs of God coming to us from earth, in mineral, and vegetation. He leaves us not in darkness, nor withholds no good things from us. God planting and growing us together; the word in the mind, and Christ all over us."[68] His interpretation of the entrails of a chicken representing three-heads-in-one was that it was one of God's strange acts.[69] Another object from nature, the root[70] of a tree in the shape of an animal's head, which appeared to have been mutilated, represented, for Mason, the world's distress (Figure 2).[71]

In Mason's preaching, he referred to objects that specifically confirm the soon return of Christ. One object was a potato resembling a human figure (Figure 3).[72] Mason tied a string around the part of the potato that resembled the neck. This object, another token of the world's distress, was interpreted by him to mean that humanity was held in bondage by wickedness, from which only God is able to deliver.[73] Another set of objects were the trunks of two saplings (i.e., young trees just beginning to grow): one appeared to resemble a human foot and the other a human hand (Figure 4).[74] Rendering an interpretation of these objects, Mason said: "God's way is a rebuke to men and He is cutting off. He is judging the world with His understanding, making the earth acknowledge His coming... God is cutting off sham church worship... It's God's time to cut off His children from worldliness, setting them apart in His will, baptized in the Christ mind."[75] Examining another object, the limb of a tree in the likeness of a crushed serpent, Mason gave the following interpretation: "We are all familiar with the trouble on the earth today caused by the subtlety of the serpent. But thank God, he said the seed of the woman should bruise the serpent's head and greatly rejoice in the power given the seed of the woman (our Savior Jesus) who is the tramping Lion of Judah."[76] The sign of the injured serpent is evidence of the ultimate triumph of Christ over the forces of evil in the world.

Mason used a variety of objects in order to preach about the nature of God and sanctification. He regarded holy living as a mystery, not as anything unknowable, but as something rarely understood by all persons and therefore requiring explanation. Signs reveal why and how persons are to live holy. One sign, part of a tree in the likeness of a dog missing one leg, was an admonition to live holy (Figure 5).[77] Concerning this object, Mason said: "Brethren, you may be apparently standing but soon you are to fall because there is something lacking in your foundation. This dog is on three legs. Take heed, my brethren, love Jesus."[78] The "dog spirit," according to Mason, is uncontrollable lust, predatory behavior, preying upon the innocent, greed, and dishonesty.[79] Not only is the dog spirit evil, it leads to the downfall of persons who become possessed by it.

Concerning another sign, a potato (four-in-one in its growth), Mason spoke about the mystery of Christ and the believer's relationship to Him. He gave the following interpretation from the potato:

Joined to Christ in the way.
Joined to Christ all day.
Joined to Christ by the word.
Joined to Christ one Lord.

Joined to Christ to sin no more.
Joined in Him to grow.
Joined to wait on the Lord.
Joined to come to His call.
Joined in Christ in the heart.
Joined with Him to have a part.
Joined to the "hallelujahs," amen!
Joined to Him like coming again.
Joined in wisdom unto Him.
Joined in love I come again.[80]

The potato, with growth in several directions, is suggestive of the multiple experiences, mostly good and enriching, of the believer in Christ.

Mason spoke further of the mystery of God and the believer's relationship to God by using the sign of an apple. The following message is his interpretation of an apple: "The apple a completeness of God's own glory. None but Jesus so sweet. What is the sign of the apple to me? A wonder of the Lord complete. The blessing of the Lord to give. I see the beauty of the apple in the word. Baptized into the wonder of Him; into His how to do; sanctified in Christ; enriched."[81]

Using the apple, he ascribes beauty, delight, and satisfaction to the human experience of the divine.

In another sign drawn from animal life, Mason found a lesson on appropriate moral and religious behavior. Mason stated: "The birds are getting their call from God. In the morning they give Him glory. They fly to His honor, singing His praises, satisfied with their portion. The bird governor is providing things. They are doing the will of the Lord."[82] The birds are a sign on how to live in obedience and praise to God. With a proper reading of signs, a person could, according to Mason, be knowledgeable of God's nature and God's will that human beings live holy.

CONCLUSION

The aspects of traditional Black preaching that receive greater attention include: call-and-response, celebration, storytelling, oratory, dramatic performance, chanting or "whooping," imagery and metaphor, use of vernacular, and concerns about social justice.[83]

While most scholars of Black preaching acknowledge it as an art with deep associations with African American culture, an area that requires further investigation is the mutual influence between preaching and other forms of folk culture, such as traditions of conjure (magic for harm or healing), "doctoring" (use of herbs, roots, and practical therapies for healing), and beliefs about the supernatural, of which the lore and practices around signs represent but one category of belief among several other spiritual beliefs. In addition to signs, other sacred folk beliefs include beliefs about God, the devil, spirits, and life after death. The modest aim of this article is to model a "thick" description of African American religion and culture, as a model for contextual study that shows possible influences and connections of rural life in the American South, Black folk culture, and Pentecostal theology in Mason's use of signs in his teaching and preaching.

Charles Harrison Mason's adaptation of the Southern folk belief in signs to biblical themes (such as the imminent return of Christ, sanctification, the visitation of God's wrath upon sinful humanity, and God's mercy) facilitated greatly the growth of Pentecostalism among persons with rural backgrounds in the South and other places where Black Southerners migrated. Because the people lived close to the land, Mason's use of signs from nature captured the attention of his listeners. The early growth of Pentecostalism cannot be attributed solely to its appeal to the poor, disinherited, disaffected, or disillusioned. Skillful preachers like Mason, with a keen insight into the gospel message of transformation and empowerment through the Holy Spirit and great facility in the folk traditions of the masses, aided its growth.

The Church of God in Christ is regarded as one of the fastest-growing denominations and largest Pentecostal groups in the United States. At a time when the Church of God in Christ is receiving greater media and public attention, it is imperative that the denomination's founder and traditions be better understood. This article has focused only on the founder's unique style of preaching rooted in Black Southern folk culture. Mason's use of objects in nature might serve as a point from which Pentecostals may engage in dialogue and debate with other persons and groups about the theology of nature.

The Church of God in Christ has always had an interest in nature. The denomination was formed in the United States at a time when most persons lived in rural farming communities. Many of the pioneer saints were first-generation city-dwellers. Having lived close to the land, they had a keen insight into the Lord Jesus Christ's parables. In the Lord's parables, he talks frequently about caring for animals, pruning vines and trees, and planting and harvesting crops. The pioneer saints could understand these sorts of things based on their personal experience. Even Mason, regarded as the founder of the denomination, was born and spent the early years of his life on a farm. Over the course of Mason's ministry, he often used events and objects from nature as illustrations for his sermons and to teach basic truths about Holiness and Pentecostalism. While God's ultimate revelation is Jesus Christ, as Mason taught and preached, God communicates with us through nature.

[Figure 1.] Bishop Charles Harrison Mason, founder of the Church of God in Christ, poses with unusually formed objects used as illustrations in his sermons. The same photograph appears in Britton 1994: 29.
A similar photograph appears also in Cornelius 1975: 14.

[Figure 2.] Bishop Mason holds a wooden object in the shape of an animal skull. The same photograph appears in the Coffey [1926] 1991: title page.

[Figure 3.] A potato resembling a human figure.
The same photograph appears in Patterson et al. 1969: x.
The photograph appears also in Mason [1924] 1987: 15.

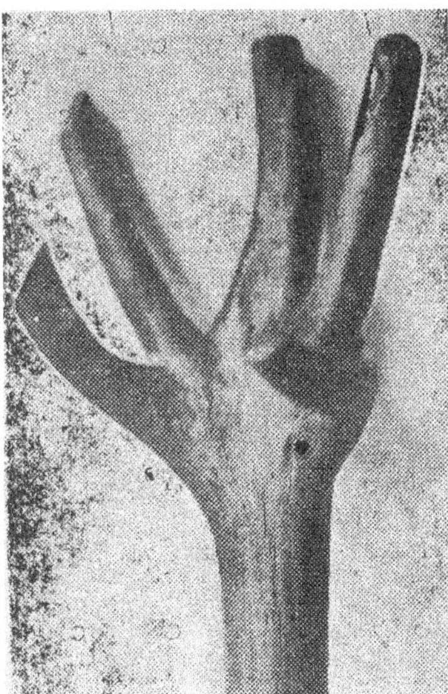

[Figure 4.] A wooden object resembling a human hand.
The same photograph appears in Patterson et al. 1969: xii.
The photograph appears also in Mason [1924] 1987: 17.

[Figure 5.] A wooden object resembling a dog with three legs only.
The same photograph appears in Coffey [1926] 1991: 8.

5

Bishop Charles Harrison Mason

The Apostle of Reconciliation

Robert R. Owens

The first sermon Elder Charles Harrison Mason preached, in 1893 in Preston, Arkansas, dealt with the subject of Holiness, which at that time was a new doctrine within the religious landscape of America. This sermon convicted people of their sins and converted many to the Gospel of Jesus Christ. Here at the beginning of his ministry the future Bishop Mason also taught that sin was the cause of all sickness and disease.[1]

The ministry of another member of the Baptist Church, Charles Price Jones (1865–1947), who was the pastor of Mt. Helm Baptist Church in Jackson, Mississippi, brought Mason deeper into Holiness teachings. Jones undertook "deeper spiritual labors"[2] in an effort to propagate the belief in Christian perfection among the members of a nascent evolving Black Baptist Convention. Jones and Mason taught the Wesleyan doctrine of "Complete or Total" sanctification[3] as a second, definite work of grace subsequent to salvation. They based these teachings on Matthew 5:48, "Therefore you shall be perfect, just as your Father in heaven is perfect."[4] These Holiness teachings became the cause for debate and divisiveness within the bounds of the nascent Calvinistic National Baptist Convention that was evolving during this same period.

After Jones convened his first Holiness convention at Mt. Helm Baptist Church at Jackson, Mississippi, on June 6, 1897, Mason and Jones became co-laborers along with John A. Jeter and Walter S. Pleasant, and worked tirelessly to spread the Holiness doctrine among the tri-state region of Mississippi, Arkansas, and Tennessee.[5] They formulated themselves as a movement, not seeking to become an organized denomination. They called themselves the Church of God movement. They soon found themselves sought after as speakers throughout the mid-South.

In March 1897, Elder Mason made a covenant with God. At the time, he was an itinerant Holiness preacher. Walking down a street in Little Rock, Arkansas, in 1897, Mason recalled he heard God say, "If you take this name, the Church of God in Christ, there will never be a building large enough to house the people I will send you."[6] Mason accepted this as direction from God and consequently proposed to C.P. Jones that they accept the name Church of God in Christ for the new Holiness church. It was a name that C.P. Jones readily accepted to identify and distinguish his organization from other Holiness groups that were propagating the faith throughout the mid-South.

The influence and reputations of the two young evangelists grew until 1899, when the nascent National Baptist Convention expelled them because of their Holiness teachings.[7] Having previously founded the Church of God in Christ (1897), they proceeded to establish this as a separate denomination, with C.P. Jones as the General Overseer, Mason as the Overseer of Tennessee, Jeter as the overseer of Arkansas, and Pleasant assisting Jones with the work in Mississippi.[8] *[An interesting sidebar to this generally accepted and oft-cited statement is the fact that to my knowledge there is no record of the Church of God in Christ being legally incorporated prior to 1922 in Tennessee. The evidence to support this assertion will be presented later in this chapter.]*

In 1907, Mason, Jeter, and David J. Young, at the request of C.P. Jones and representing the new fledgling denomination, visited the Azusa Street Revival in Los Angeles to inquire about the new teaching of Baptism of the Holy Spirit. Once there they received the experience of the Baptism of the Holy Spirit accompanied by the initial evidence of speaking in tongues.[9] This was a life-changing event in young Mason's life and ministry. Upon receiving this newfound blessing of the baptism of the Holy Spirit, Mason remained on in Los Angeles, where he was indoctrinated in the faith, accepting the theological position espoused by Elder William J. Seymour (1872–1922), leader of the Azusa Street Mission. This theology, derived from the teachings of Charles F. Parham (1873–1929), taught that speaking in tongues constituted the "*Only*" initial evidence of the Baptism with the Holy Ghost.[10]

Leaving Azusa Street, instead of going directly home to Memphis, Tennessee, Mason traveled to the tidewater area of Virginia.[11] According to oral traditions, this was an area where he had long been an active apostle.[12] He stopped first at a small Holiness church he had previously brought into his fast-growing network of believers in the Chuckatuck area of Suffolk County, Friendship Cathedral, where he preached the Baptism of the Holy Ghost.

A revival broke out in response to his preaching in which many people gave their lives to the Lord, and received the Pentecostal Baptism amidst great excitement. News spread from tobacco fields to peanut fields in the rural areas of Southeast Virginia. People came from as far away as Norfolk and the church in Chuckatuck was greatly increased. At this time, Elder Mason told the people they should refrain from the activities going on for the 300th anniversary of the founding of Jamestown. He also told them that if they would instead fast and pray the Lord would greatly bless the saints and the city of Norfolk.[13]

After leaving Chuckatuck, Elder Mason and several other leaders from that area traveled to Norfolk to spread the new Pentecostal message. The first place they went was the old Grant Street Church, where he usually attended when visiting the Tidewater area. After he preached a sermon on the Baptism of the Holy Ghost and shared about his experiences at Azusa Street, the leaders asked him and his companions to leave that church.[14]

Bishop Mason was about to continue on to Memphis when he felt compelled by the Holy Ghost to stay and continue spreading the message of Pentecost. Having no church open to him, he started a street ministry in downtown Norfolk in April 1907. Mason preached on the street outside the Ferry Terminal on Commercial Place. This built on an earlier work done by Lucy Farrow, one of the pioneer evangelists to leave Azusa Street for Africa. This mighty woman of God had preached the Pentecostal message in Portsmouth and Norfolk in 1906.[15]

Many people scorned and ridiculed Mason when he started preaching on the street. The police threatened him with arrest, but they never did carry out this threat. In addition, although this was in the darkest days of America's Apartheid and its legislative enforcers, the Jim Crow Laws, numerous Caucasians attended the meetings and responded to Mason's call for salvation, sanctification, and Baptism of the Holy Ghost. Estimates of the number saved during this 1907 revival vary between 6,000,[16] several thousand,[17] and 600.[18] The variance in these figures aptly represents the numerous contradictions found in many of the early reports and stories based upon different streams of oral traditions.

After the street preaching had gathered in this large number of converts, both African American and Caucasian, Mason started holding meetings in private homes, which, despite the rabid prejudice of the times, retained this inter-racial component. As more and more people continued to respond to the Pentecostal message, they soon needed larger facilities. Staying in Norfolk, he first rented a storefront on Monticello Avenue, then a larger one on St. Paul Street, and then a still larger one on Cumberland Street. Before Elder Mason left for Memphis, he organized the saints who had been saved in the revival into a church with himself as the pastor. Within a short space of time they purchased a lot on Goff Street and built the first church, which was to become the C.H. Mason Memorial Church of God in Christ. This church is now known as the "Mother" church because it has been the seedbed for so many preachers, pastors, bishops, and churches.[19]

Mason finally felt "led" by the Holy Ghost to continue his journey home to Memphis. He arrived in Memphis in late July, just in time to visit his own church and to prepare to make his way to the Holy Convocation of the Church of God in Christ for 1907. Mason was surprised to find that he was not the first person to preach the message of Azusa Street to his own congregation in Memphis. Upon reaching home he discovered that he was preceded by Glen Cook (1867–1948), a veteran of the great Revival who had served as Elder Seymour's business manager. Brother Cook, a Caucasian, was in the middle of a cross-country evangelistic tour spreading the word of the Pentecostal blessing.[20] While Mason was away, Cook, Leonard Adams, B.B. Cashwell, and Mack M. Pinson, all Caucasian brothers, visited Mason's church and brought great report of the Baptism of the Holy Spirit experience.

It was at the 1907 Convocation that Mason presented his case for the Baptism of the Holy Ghost, as taught at Azusa Street by Elder W.J. Seymour. General Overseer of the Church of God in Christ, C.P. Jones, opposed his efforts at the convocation in August of 1907 in Jackson, Mississippi. The General Overseer "regarded the new Holy Ghost experience of speaking in tongues as a delusion."[21] C.P. Jones thought that COGIC should remain strictly a Holiness church, rejecting the new Pentecostal teachings, thus forming a united front with other Holiness denominations such as the Church of God (Anderson, Ind.), The Salvation Army, The Christian and Missionary Alliance, and the Nazarene Church[22] against what was thought to be a dangerous innovation.

Mason attempted to lead the entire Church of God in Christ into the new Pentecostal mold, but Jones, who controlled the Convocation, demanded that Mason soften his position to say that speaking in tongues was merely "one" of the initial evidences of the Baptism with the Holy Ghost.[23] Mason refused to do this, so the General Overseer and the Convocation "withdrew from C.H. Mason and all who promulgated the doctrine of speaking with tongues the right hand of fellowship."[24]

When Mason left the Convocation approximately, half of the delegates went with him. Mason then sent out a letter to all the members of the Church telling them of his experience and asking that they meet with him in Memphis in September of 1907.[25] This meeting was convened as the "Pentecostal Assembly of the Church of God in Christ."[26] At this meeting, the delegates elected Mason as the Chief Apostle of the Church.[27] This Assembly also amended the Articles of Religion of the Church by adding a "Pentecostal paragraph."[28] COGIC at the same time retained a belief in Sanctification. This Holiness-Pentecostal mix was expressed in a statement added to the official manual of the church: "We, therefore, believe that before a believer can be filled with the Holy Ghost, he must first be sanctified."[29]

With these actions, the split between the Holiness and the Pentecostal wings of the Church of God in Christ became permanent. A court battle raged for two years to decide which faction had the exclusive right to use the name and charter of the church.[30] The court of Shelby County, Tennessee, decided in favor of the Pentecostal Assembly on May 15, 1909. According to an article entitled "Opinion" that appeared in *The Whole Truth* (April 1968), this ruling was based upon the fact (in direct contravention of what has come to be the generally accepted "Common Knowledge") that the Church of God in Christ was not at that time legally incorporated:

> It is insisted on behalf of the complainants that the church to which the defendants and complainants belong is a member of an association of churches under control of a superior council… It has

> no authority whatever over the individual churches. Its action can only be in any case advisory.
>
> Indeed we do not think that any council has ever been organized. It appears that in January 1906, there was a meeting of ministers of various colored churches professing sanctification; and there was again a meeting in August 1906. At this meeting there was present the pastor of the church of South Wellington Street Memphis, [Mason] which is the subject of the present controversy and also a member–one Murphy. The evidence, however, fails to show that either of these persons was commissioned to place the church under the authority of the alleged superior council, nor does it appear that there was such authority conferred upon other person present.
>
> It appears that the two meetings in Jackson, Mississippi, above referred to were what are called "holiness" meetings composed largely of ministers of that persuasion. It is true that while these men were present, they undertook to effect some kind of organization and appointed three men whom they called overseers, C. P. Jones' supposed jurisdiction was the State of Mississippi, Mason's, the State of Tennessee, Jeter's the State of Arkansas. Their powers, according to Jones, consisted principally in watching over the churches and seeing that no improper ministers officiated. It required two of them to authorize a minister to act as such, and it seems they assumed the authority to dispose of ministers also.
>
> We cannot find in the record any sufficient evidence that this authority was conferred upon these men by the churches. We are likewise unable to find in the record any sufficient evidence that the alleged superior council had conferred upon it any authority by the churches; certainly not by the congregation whose church is in controversy in the present case.
>
> We think the overwhelming weight of evidence shows that the defendants' [Mason's] church belongs to the congregational order, and that it is not subject to oversight by any superior ecclesiastical organization.[31]

Consequently, it is precisely because the Church was *not* incorporated at the time of this dispute that Mason was able to maintain control of the name Church of God in Christ. The Holiness wing of the church is now reorganized as the Church of Christ (Holiness) U.S.A.[32]

Mason insisted on retaining the worship and prayer traditions of slave religion, which included the prayer circle and lively worship (such as shouting, jumping, and the "Holy Dance"), but, at the same time, he led the church in developing a new Pentecostal spirituality.[33] Mason's leadership moved COGIC from the inward focus on personal perfection of the Holiness Movement to an outward focus that saw the social suffering of the oppressed as something that the Christian community should address and ameliorate. COGIC grew rapidly after the split and was soon the largest African American Pentecostal denomination in the world.[34]

Although "the Church of God in Christ saw a link between religious practice and racial identity,"[35] Elder Mason, deeply affected by his experience of the profoundly inter-racial revival at Azusa Street,[36] welcomed the many White ministers who were routinely thrown out of their churches and denominations once they had received the Baptism of the Holy Spirit. After Mason won the court battles, he led the way in COGIC's reorganization as a legally recognized church. Thus the clergy who held credentials authorized by the new denomination were able to obtain railway passes, and perform marriages and other official functions.[37] Reaching across the racial divide, Bishop Mason "[t]hrough his practice of ordaining ministers of all races...acted as a conduit for the fire of the Azusa Street Revival to all parts of the United States."[38]

Mason is considered "a race-transcending prophet–someone who never forgot the significance of race but refused to be confined to a race."[39] Although highly unusual for the times, this aspect of the reorganized Church of God in Christ manifested itself in the fact that between 1907 and 1914 Bishop Mason ordained 350 White ministers.[40] As a result of this practice, between 1907 and 1914 there came to be as many White ministers in COGIC as there were African American. "At times, Mason referred to the White group of ministers in the Church of God in Christ as the 'White work of the Church.'"[41] But, sadly, "By 1913 it had become increasingly clear that as Pentecostals moved toward denominationalism, they would follow the segregating practices of American culture."[42] However, this tendency to accept and amplify the prevailing sin of the surrounding culture did not come from above. Bishop Mason continued to minister to and serve the Caucasian segment of the church even as they planned to divide the church.

In 1913 elders E.N. Bell (1866–1923) and H.A. Goss (1883–1864) sent invitations stating that a general council of "all pentecostal saints and Churches of God in Christ"[43] would convene in April 1914 in Hot Springs, Arkansas. "This invitation went only to the White saints. E.N. Bell's periodical, *Word and Witness*, was not distributed in the black religious community."[44] Following this call and the meetings that flowed from it, the majority of COGIC's White ministers left in 1914, forming the Assemblies of God. One can only wonder what lens was used to study these events that prompted Historian Robert M. Anderson to state that "no hostility, racial or other seems to have been involved"[45] in this split. The only evidence Anderson presents of this attitude, "Bishop Mason addressed that organizing meeting and gave his blessing to the new denomination,"[46] appears to express Mason's accommodating attitude toward the seceding White clergy. However, it does not reveal the attitude of those who left, except collaterally in that they invited him to speak. Another indication of Bishop Mason's view of race relations within the church can be seen in one of his favorite sayings: "The church is like the eye: it has a little black in it and a little white in it, and without both it can't see."[47]

Bishop Ithiel Clemmons addressed the issue of why the Whites left by stating, "According to white scholars, they left because the larger society, especially in the South, refused to modify its worship patterns to accommodate whites. Moreover, whites became restive when they could not assume the prevailing leadership role."[48] Clemmons also states that "White American Pentecostalism and Neo-Pentecostalism, at least since 1914, employed segregationist politics and racist attitudes similar to those of greater North American society."[49]

Addressing the impact of this exodus of Whites from COGIC, Vinson Synan says, "The formation of the Assemblies of God was of crucial importance to the future development of the Pentecostal movement, effectively marking the end of a notable experiment in interracial development."[50] Burgess, McGee, and Alexander sum up the desertion of the Whites by paraphrasing Frank Bartleman's famous quote, "The color line that had been washed away in the blood of Jesus at the Azusa Street revival reappeared."[51]

When the beloved Bishop Mason died on November 17, 1961, he had led the denomination he had founded for longer (1897–1961) than any other religious organizational leader in American

History.[52] His long service at the helm left an indelible mark, as the church he loved and labored over for so long continues to stand at the forefront of those seeking an end to racial discrimination as they follow in the footsteps of Bishop C.H. Mason, the Apostle of Reconciliation.

6

The Church of God in Christ Transforms Women's Ministries Through the Positive Influence of Chief Apostle Bishop C. H. Mason

Glenda Williams Goodson

A male elder once said to me that if the women of the Church of God in Christ (COGIC) withheld their finances, support, and loyalty for only one month, real dialogue would immediately develop regarding women in ministry and anything else the sisters wished to discuss. As I laughed along with him, I thought that statement very revealing regarding the tremendous spiritual authority and financial prowess of COGIC women. It was the women who provided COGIC founder Bishop Charles Harrison Mason "standing with the banks" with a donation of $168, a tremendous sum for Black people in the early twentieth century. Success indicators of this type document that women understood his vision of an army of believers going into "the everywhere" spreading the gospel. And although developing power of this kind was not a simple undertaking, with shared vision and tenacity the women strategically nurtured their leader's vision to become what is arguably the largest female-led ministry in the United States.

Given America's systemic patriarchal mentality of the early twentieth century, what were the origins of this strong women's ministry? How did denominational women develop bands, units, and auxiliaries that very successfully advanced the cause of Jesus Christ? Answers may be found by examining COGIC's early development, with emphasis on evaluating the role of women's ministry. However, one must view this expansion through a lens that takes into consideration their solid backing by Mason within the confines of his day. This essay examines how Mason, while not ordaining women, positively impacted the lives of female constituents by personally influencing and supporting early female leaders. These pioneers maintained a reverence for Jesus Christ and a commitment to Mason's teachings as they partnered with others who wished to see the life-changing love of Jesus Christ expand throughout the world.

In my book, *I Commend Unto You Phebe: Female Leader-Activists in the Missionary Societies and Ministries of the African American Church 1900–1925*, I included the ignored voices of sainted COGIC heroines who prayerfully moved through rural and (as they migrated northward) urban communities proclaiming the gospel while forging a legacy of organizational, educational, and financial expertise in domestic and undeveloped foreign fields. Rather than bemoan racist, sexist, and classist systems, they lifted their sisters and their church to new levels of excellence while retaining Holiness principles. This paper challenges future COGIC female leaders to build upon the foundation for which their foremothers so willingly sacrificed. In the dawn of the twenty-first century, there are innumerable lessons to be learned. Like our foremothers, we must not forget that for which we labor–winning, nurturing, and discipling individuals for whom Christ died. These giants' biblically based moral authority challenges us to "*live lives worthy of God, Who calls us into His kingdom and glory*" (1 Thess. 2:12, NIV).

Introduction

The Church of God in Christ, led by former Baptist ministers Elder Charles Price Jones and Elder Charles Harrison Mason, was first organized in 1897 as a Holiness church. After Mason's Spirit baptism at the Azusa Street Revival (Los Angeles 1906–1909), Mason and Jones parted ways over the issue of glossolalia. The COGIC then reorganized in 1907 as a Holiness-Pentecostal body that believed in the Baptism of the Holy Ghost with the sign of speaking in tongues, with Mason as General Overseer and Chief Apostle. In the early twentieth century, COGIC's emphasis on the outward manifestation of inward holiness by stressing changed lifestyles, calling women to dress modestly, and retaining distinct Afrocentric worship customs was novel. Mason's approach was to preach radically, and after adopting the Pentecostal doctrine of Holy Ghost Baptism, the church successfully turned communities upside down, eventually becoming America's largest Pentecostal church.[1] Little narrative is found on the legacy of women in the growth of COGIC. Therefore, this essay provides exposition of COGIC's female-centered heritage and summarizes how COGIC's founder's unique leadership style positively modeled Christ's example in utilizing the talents of every individual to spread the gospel of God.

Despite subordination to secondary leadership roles, women were open to having a role in the new organization's growth. Mason's keen insight linked the West African dual sex system firmly to the foundational structure of the new movement. Adrienne Israel notes many West African women wielded authority in spiritual as well as domestic affairs:

> To institutionalize their power they formed solidarity groups from which they gained a strong "psychological sense of self-esteem." Some West African societies ensured women political power...by developing what anthropologists have called a "dual-sex" system. Women's councils not only governed women's affairs but their representatives voiced women's interests from the village to the king's court. Although the dual-sex system gave prominence to women in community affairs, they remained, as a group, subservient to husbands.[2]

Despite the dehumanizing view of Black women as servile, obstinate, or brazen, Mason's courage shines through in that he acted upon his belief in shared power. Mason used his influence to preserve the tradition of female authority by establishing a strong Women's Department led by Lizzie Woods Robinson. Despite opposition, he would not allow the women to be intimidated but laid a strategic foundation of inclusive permeation throughout the church and community. In one noteworthy instance, when Robinson's leadership role was challenged by the men, Mason refused to allow these pastors to diminish Robinson's leadership role. His instructions to the men opposing Robinson's authority to teach men as well as women was to "sit down, and learn some sense."[3] Further, by establishing the Women's Department shortly after COGIC's reorganization, Mason aligned himself with the Apostle Paul's teaching in Galatians 3:27–29. His contract with the women, beginning with the Overseer of Women (National Mother) position, facilitated a new paradigm for the transformation of their role as the church rapidly spread throughout the globe. Cheryl Sanders writes:

> The emergence of the COGIC Women's Department was timely in view of the plight of Black women in the church [authoritarian style demanded by the nature of the episcopal polity: hierarchical, individualistic, and dominating] and society [at a time when employment for black women was primarily restricted to domestic service at low wages, the Department presented "professional" roles for Black working women], during the first decade of the twentieth century… The spiritual and professional focus of this organization of black women produced significant affirmations of Black female personhood.[4]

After his dynamic encounter with the Holy Spirit at the Azusa Street Revival in 1906, and subsequent reorganization of COGIC, Mason's charismatic leadership and organizational genius were stamped indelibly on every aspect of the church's life and witness.[5] Characteristics of organizations, whether successful or not, can be found in the development of any institution. In successful organizations, the leader, often a visionary, uses resources within his or her power to create a common vision and empower followers to propel the institution forward. According to Marilyn Loden, "[W]ithin every organization, people respond to new ideas in distinct and predictable ways, based on differences in individual tolerance and perceived risk. Behavioral scientists categorize variations in individual response to new ideas into five distinct response groups. One's placement in a particular segment is based on the level of perceived opportunity and risk."[6] Mason scores high in two of the five groups as an innovator (2.5 percent) and change agent (13.5 percent). What is extraordinary in the Mason leadership model is that many change agents were women such as Lizzie Robinson, Lillian Coffey, and Arenia Mallory, who were used in leading positions to advance the church's worldview.

By the early twentieth century, women were ready to act as change agents. Many African Americans continued to experience hardship and poverty, but now looked beyond merely surviving to explore new opportunities. Change agent Mary McCloud Bethune founded the Daytona Normal and Industrial Institute for Girls, where she taught self-responsibility, respect for self and community, and, like her National Council of Negro Women, urged a generation to lift others as they climbed. Black women, continuously challenged with both sexist and racist practices, partnered with sympathetic White women. Paradoxically, while exploring these tenable partnerships, decisions made by well-meaning White women became part of the culture of disenfranchisement: women of color led by the likes of Ida B. Wells-Barnett and Mary Church Terrell joined marchers for a parade outside the White House in 1913. Parade organizer Alice Paul made a political decision to request them to move to the back of the parade after resistance from Southerners whose support was needed for congressional passage of the Suffrage Amendment.[7] (Terrell marched at the back but Wells-Barnett refused and joined the White Illinois delegation.) Even after ratification after 1920, Southern Black women who attempted to vote experienced physical and economic intimidation, poll taxes, educational and character requirements, and were excluded from the Democratic primary.[8] What were Black women to do given this hostile climate? Since the awakening revivals during slavery, the Black church has always played an important role in the life of community. It was in the refuge of the Black church they found a place to articulate and develop goals for empowerment. COGIC female pioneers saw in Mason's charismatic ministry a foundation of prayer, healing, and deliverance as a venue to present their gifts back to God by strategically bridging their historical roles as nurturers, healers, and pray-ers of the family.

Mason's respect for his female constituency's God-given abilities transformed male leaders, some of whom entered COGIC from traditional mainline churches where women held limited ecclesial power. Part of the back-story has been to trace subtle psychological nuances by which women got things done in a patriarchal system that lifted men up and held women down. In allowing early bishops and pastors the opportunity to collaborate with female leaders, COGIC quickly became America's premier Pentecostal church. The question to ask is how Mason's leadership style changed the women's vision of reality. This examination offers a glimpse of early leaders directly influenced by the personal contact, direct coaching, and mentoring of Mason, namely those who served during the first three general supervisors' watches: Lizzie Woods Robinson, Lillian Brooks Coffey, and Annie Pennington Bailey.[9]

MASON'S KEY LEARNINGS FROM EARLY CHILDHOOD IMPACT BLACK WOMEN

In 1890, the U.S. Census recorded the U.S. population to be 62,947,714, of which 7,488,676 (11.9 percent) were African American. In the context of the social milieu, the decade of the 1890s was a hotbed of upward mobility. Blacks could boast that much progress had been made twenty-five years after Emancipation: two of the first African American banks opened (Savings Bank of the Grand Fountain United Order of the Reformers, Richmond, Virginia, and Capital Savings Bank, Washington, D.C.), several Baptist organizations combined to form the National Baptist Convention USA, and Booker T. Washington became the first principal of Tuskegee Institute. Black women made strides when Mary Church Terrell founded the National Association of Colored Women in 1896.[10]

In the years prior to the formation of COGIC, the Mississippi Plan, approved on November 1, used literacy and "understanding" tests to disenfranchise Blacks, including educators. Similar statutes were adopted by South Carolina (1895) and Louisiana (1898), with North Carolina, Alabama, Virginia, Georgia, and Oklahoma adopting after 1897). From 1894–1897 almost five hundred lynchings were recorded, the great abolitionist Frederick Douglas died (1895); and Jim Crow laws were legally enacted through Plessy v. Ferguson.[11] In this world of chaos for Blacks, a courageous duo, Charles Price Jones and Charles Harrison Mason, founded COGIC in 1897.[12] It stands to reason that Mason, son of former slaves, shared a sense of social concern about the conditions of the day. According to Clemmons, "Mason had gone to the Azusa Street revival very much aroused about the social conditions in the South, especially the lynchings, the mistreatment of Ida B. Wells at the hands of Whites in Memphis, the pervasiveness of deep poverty among Blacks and Whites, the KKK, Blacks' inability to vote, and the ungodly deeds among the races."[13]

Mason's worldview changed radically after Azusa. Not only did Christian beliefs and the Holiness lifestyle offer possibilities for sanctification but Christ also made available power to change lives so that Blacks could compete in this social context. Nevertheless, there were crises, which, after overcome, would jump-start the movement to invade the entire South and then spread northward. After receiving the Baptism of the Holy Ghost at Azusa, Mason and his longtime co-laborer and friend Jones parted over the issue of speaking in tongues. It is important to note that while Mason spoke with tongues as *confirmation* of Holy Ghost Baptism, it was the *impartation* of the Spirit that Mason and others sought.[14] Israel says that after it adopted the Pentecostal teaching on tongues (glossolalia), the COGIC began to attract spiritual seekers from the dominant church groups. As Baptist and Methodist women began to join the denomination in large numbers, their work needed structure.[15]

One of Mason's resolves was to preserve elements of slave religion, which may have been a determining factor in the formation of the women's ministry. The slave heritage included two essential elements that Mason carried over into the denomination: (1) the principle of spiritual equality, which allowed women free expression of their spiritual gifts, and (2) the ideal of shared social responsibility in which women worked side by side with men in community life, as well as in the fields. West African (and later slave) traditions allowed women to wield authority in spiritual and civil matters, but preserved ultimate authority for a male leader: the father in the slave home and the male pastor in the slave church. The structure that the COGIC developed to involve women in the work of the ministry strikingly resembles the West African dual-sex system model in principle and form.[16] There is no research whether Mason's parents, Jerry and Eliza Mason, modeled this system or how his mother's role shaped his view of women's roles. Clemmons says she prayed fervently for her son and while a young boy Mason "prayed earnestly with his mother, asking above all things for God to give him a religion like the one he had heard about from the old slaves and seen demonstrated in their lives."[17] In this context Mason would later spur an entire generation of women to play leading roles in the church's growth. The first to organize the women's ministry under Mason's tutelage was Lizzie Woods Robinson.

Lizzie Robinson, Overseer of Women's Work (1860–1945)

Jesus saw the giftings and potential of women at the beginning of His ministry–e.g., in Galilee, women gathered in the upper room and received the same power as men on the Day of Pentecost and the Apostle Paul commended women who labored with him.[18] Mason also saw women as equal partners in ministry. Although society imposed a substandard citizenship upon them as Black and female,

Mason caused them to frame their worldview on possibilities and potential. The positive coaching from "the little big man" from the South helped them to rise out of obscurity to realize great achievements in education, build structures such as the National Headquarters, and, most of all, make great strides in church work.

By 1911, the women's work had started with 20-year-old Lillian Brooks already a singing evangelist. Records indicate that Mason had searched for a woman capable of directing the women's work and may have had someone else in mind, but the name of Lizzie Woods was continuously brought to his attention.[19] Woods was a former slave born April 5, 1860, to Moses Smith and Elizabeth Jackson. By the time she was five years old, the Civil War had ended and her father was dead. As a young girl she heard a voice calling, "Liz, Liz, Liz." From the age of eight on she read Scriptures to her mother and friends. Later she was sanctified after reading Joanna Moore's *Hope* magazine. Established in 1885, through *Hope* Moore built a network of women who provided training in Bible study, reading, and home schooling.[20] As more women became acquainted with the publication, Bible Bands sprung up across the South, with Woods proving an impressive organizer. Observing her leadership abilities, Moore persuaded the missionary society of the American Baptists to send her to the Baptist Training Academy in Dermott, Arkansas, for two years. Soon she was appointed the Academy's matron. Mason met her while conducting a meeting at the Academy. After teaching about the Baptism of the Holy Ghost, she was filled and immediately "disfellowshiped" from the Baptist Church.[21] Mason appointed her General Overseer of Women's Work during the 1911 convocation. At Mason's 1961 funeral, Ida Baker, the daughter of Lizzie Robinson (Woods later married Edward Robinson[22]) recalls, "Bishop Charles Harrison Mason didn't overlook anybody. After he had preached out and got a congregation of brethren he decided it was nice to take the women since they were the mothers of the generations then and to come, he reached and got my mother..."[23] Mason's use of the term Overseer of Women's Work may have been intended to note that a separate work for the women was to be recognized. Butler suggests, "The term 'overseer,' used in the New Testament to designate a bishop, was bestowed on Robinson to solidify her appointment over all women's activities. In effect, Mason made Robinson a bishop over COGIC women."[24] Robinson described her job as having the "general supervision over all the women's work, and to evangelize and systematize the work among the women."[25] After discovering two major groups of women working in the church–one praying and the other studying and teaching the Word, she merged them. This united team would become the first auxiliary of women, the Prayer and Bible Band. The work would explode to include the birth of auxiliaries and units as the Women's Department developed a formal structure.

Mason's Alliance with Women Builds Partnerships For Growth

Led by Robinson, the women of the movement were vital to its expansion and were ready to give up things dear to them to be a part of the new community of believers. Ostracized, ridiculed, and persecuted, former Baptist and Methodist women made bold moves to turn away from lifelong relationships in society and the church. Initially some families attempted to dissuade the women from joining the church, then escalated their protest through excommunication. Dr. Arenia Mallory, who became President of COGIC's Saints Junior College, chose to cast her lot with the saints after her mother's ultimatum to leave the sanctified church or leave her house. Women such as Mallory saw, in Mason, God's twentieth-century representative of Pentecostalism as found in Acts 1:8–a man who totally trusted God and possessed an overarching vision of the limitless nature of God's ability to transform society. His confident knowledge of his God-given mission allowed him to project a positive leadership style that would grant Robinson, his appointee as Overseer of Women's Work, freedom to support her vision. Some male constituents resisted the idea of shared power, but the majority recognized the benefits of using all resources to gain more souls for the Kingdom. Bishop O.W. Gillespie of Southeast Illinois wrote, "I thank God how God inspired him to give the late Mother Lizzie Roberson to organize the women of the grand old Church of God in Christ and to set a profound example of liberty for the great women."[26] These men recognized the successful Mason/Robinson partnership and set about modeling their state work after the national paradigm.

The strength of COGIC women in unifying their efforts in building ministries, schools, and communities continued to be nurtured by Mason's support. In fact, Estrelda Alexander says

Mason's partnership with the women took on a distinctive character that was specifically fashioned to allow the women a degree of empowerment while maintaining strategic ecclesial authority.[27] With Mason's support and the cooperation of Robinson's traveling companions, Prayer and Bible Bands were established across the country by church mothers. As COGIC continued to burgeon, Robinson appointed women to strategic areas of ministry across the U.S. Her first State Mothers were women who had previously served her as traveling companions. These pioneer leaders were thoroughly indoctrinated in the polity of the Church: Fannie Jackson, Lucinda Bostic (Missouri, Illinois) Jessie Strickland, Nancy Gamble (Southern Illinois, Indiana), and Eliza Hollins (Louisiana). They understood that although Robinson had the power to appoint them with the approval of the state overseer, it was Mason who set the tone for their freedom to lead. They used the terms *dad*, *friend*, *encourager*, *a man with fatherly Christian conduct*, *outstanding preacher*, *great apostle*, *teacher*, *illustrious leader*, and *a man consecrated* to describe Mason. As the work of the Women's Department continued to increase, praying women with demonstrated leadership abilities were added to the ranks of State Mothers. One such woman, Supervisor L.O. Hale of California, was said to be "A School of Wisdom." Hale was baptized with the Holy Ghost in October 1914 in Los Angeles and traveled the entire State of California by bus inspiring the women. The National Mother was empowered to appoint State Supervisors and Robinson appointed Hale as Supervisor during the 1935 Convocation. She named her assistant supervisor Dr. Cora Berry, principal of the Emmanuel Bible Institute of Los Angeles; a state-supported institution of learning that boasted more than 400 students.[28]

Robinson saw that in addition to spiritual training COGIC women could be further organized to make a difference in the larger community. After meeting Elder Searcy in 1926, she invited him to Memphis, after which the Home and Foreign Mission Board was established. Organizing this vital church entity at age 65, she traveled to 40 cities covering 18 states in less than one year.[29] Working with her husband, Elder Robinson, the two "dug out" (planted) many churches traveling by foot or wagon, experiencing much suffering and very limited finances. After relocating to Omaha, they established the first COGIC in Nebraska, with the help of Lucinda Bostic and Nancy Gamble. When the Robinsons began to proclaim the Pentecostal message, mainline church leaders–including many Holiness leaders–severely criticized the doctrine of tongues. Hostility led to violence and the Robinsons suffered verbal and physical attacks.[30] In spite of hardship, the Robinsons continued to travel and spread the Pentecostal message. She and her only child, Ida Baker, were very instrumental in the mammoth World War II Mason Temple building effort until its completion and dedication. She attended the 1945 Convocation, where she walked through Mason Temple,

> looked at the work of her hands, sat in the assembly hall which bears her name, held conferences with her State Mothers, revised her constitution,...turned to Lillian Brooks Coffey, whom she had trained...to courageously lead the women on in the fear of the Lord, to stick to the Bible. She went to her room...and in a few hours drew the drapery of her couch about her and fell asleep. Thus ended the career of one of the great organizers among women and one of the oldest pioneers of the Church in Christendom.[31]

Lillian Brooks Coffey, Second General Supervisor (1891–1964)

Lillian Brooks (Coffey) was born March 29, 1891, to Jerry and Lula Brooks in Paris, Tennessee.[32] She met Mason while she was an impressionable child and looked upon him as a friend, counselor, and protector. Brooks Coffey recalled:

> My first remembrance of Bishop Charles Harrison Mason was when I was a WEE LITTLE GIRL. He was invited (as I was told in later years) into our home by my grandfather who was a Baptist minister. Brother Mason (which was a popular name to be called at that time) took up much time with...the children in the home. After the establishment of the Sunday School, Brother Mason... one Sunday morning...taught us about Jesus in a child-like manner. He got to the part of the story where Jesus...became a man and His friends killed Him. I began crying and said to Brother Mason, "I want Him to love me..." That morning the Lord touched my little tender heart and saved me. I have been in this Church

> under Bishop Mason ever since. As I grew older…I traveled…with Brother Mason and older Sisters. I sang and read the Bible as he preached… He influenced me.[33]

Coffey later worked as Secretary for Mason for 21 years as he groomed her in the protocols of the Church. His influence was so great, when she and her husband Samuel Coffey separated because of what she called her ever-expanding responsibilities in the ministry, she turned to Mason as advisor. When she divorced, Mason, who did not believe in "double marriages," instructed her not to marry again. Although there were several occasions in which she wished to marry, she complied. "He would say, 'Watch out for your future…some day you will lead the women…and anything you do now will count heavily against your leadership.'"[34] After Robinson's death, in a unanimous vote, Coffey was appointed International Supervisor in 1945 and stated "IT WAS FROM HIS MOUTH THAT I GOT MY ORDER OF THE DAY!"[35] The great Women's International Convention (WIC) founder served the Church for over 54 years. Her close ties with Mason (and indeed his molding of her thinking) may have been a key factor in allowing her the freedom to carry out some amazing accomplishments, including expanding the Women's Work to more than 20 units and organizing 17 additional auxiliaries.[36]

Coffey Establishes Women's International Convention (1950)

Coffey established Women's Departments in Illinois, Minnesota, Wisconsin, Indiana, Mississippi, and Tennessee. It was important to Mason and early leaders that seasoned women be entrusted to hold churches together until a pastor could be sent to lead churches sprouting up under the COGIC banner. Such was the case of Coffey's pioneering work in Chicago. Prior to her arrival, Elder Willis Thomas and Elder McFadden served as trailblazers before leaving the city. With the belief that a COGIC congregation "should and ought to be a great stronghold for God in the City of Chicago," she toiled to accomplish this goal with much optimism. She made plans with others to contact Elder William Roberts, then Mason's assistant pastor, stating "that we should have a church that would be second to none if Brother Willie was given an opportunity to work here."[37] Coffey held the church until Roberts made the final decision to relocate. WIC Editor Albertha McKenzie recalled, "The day finally arrived that Bishop C.H. Mason was contacted and Elder Wm. Roberts was on his way to investigate the city where many said that it was impossible for a [COGIC congregation] to be planted… Although he had been here during the year of 1915, he did not stay but went back to Memphis, for a period of almost two years, and in 1917 moved his family to the City of Chicago."[38]

In 1950, with Mason supporting her initiative, Coffey's vision of a conclave of women gathering for instruction and spiritual refreshing was realized in the establishment of the International Women's Convention, an annual event. Writing in the First Women's Convention Souvenir journal, Coffey stated, "We, the Women of the Church of God in Christ, Inc., pay the highest respect to our Founder, and Chief Apostle, Bishop Charles Harrison Mason… We appreciate the cooperation that he is giving toward the "First National Convention of the Women."[39] Bishop Louis Henry Ford assisted in organizing the first convention, hosted by Bishop S.M. Crouch of California in 1951. Coffey and her cabinet organized this convention to provide the female constituency their most unique opportunity for Christian fellowship and work with one another.[40] One hundred delegates were asked for $100 each for registration, lodging, and meals. When the famous "Coffey Train" rolled into Los Angeles, it was the beginning of the largest churchwomen's convention of the day. The theme for this first convention was "'Peace in a War-Torn World,' St. John 14:27." One of the convention's prime stated objectives was to financially assist the work of missions and education.[41] According to Elder E. Roberts' souvenir dedication:

> The dream of a "better way" and the support of missions has been shining with such luminosity… [m]aking known ONE purpose… to abolish slipshod methods, and indifferent attitudes toward Missions in this first meeting of its kind. Most wonderful for the superior achievement of a great God, thousands for Missions, 200 hearing the call. Our Dreamer came "Not to Destroy" but to fulfill a…yearning to help Missions On a Large Scale. Realizing this great purpose, no one should arrive in Cavalcade disappointed and embarrassed. For "this is that" the extra PLUS FOR MISSIONS.[42]

In planning the first convention, she was not in the best of health, but demonstrated persistence, determination, and faith in God to work with His vision to be a blessing to the people of God with a willingness to empower other women. Under Coffey's watch, the Women's Department supported twelve foreign mission posts. She raised funds for the building of the Elizabeth White Clinic in Liberia, shared in the purchase of land with Mrs. Elsie Mason for the Mason School in Haiti, purchased land for the Lillian Brooks Coffey School in Haiti, and was instrumental in the establishment of other schools and churches in British West Indies, Hawaii, England, and parts of Africa. After the 1953 Miami convention, the post-convention delegation traveled to the Bahamas, Haiti, Jamaica, and Cuba. Mother Luella Westbrook wrote, "Tuesday, May 12 at 7:45am, this delegation and many of the Saints came to the airport to bid us farewell. Mother Coffey…wanted to go so very much, but her health would not allow it. After singing…Bishop Samuel Crouch…offered prayer.[43] The group flew in on a specially chartered Pan American plane."[44]

Coffey also established a rest home, furthered the work of missions, and pioneered in the work of education. This Mason protégé learned the lessons of faith and sisterly cooperation well–that the women could accomplish anything that God placed in their hearts to do for His people. One of her most outstanding achievements was securing 154 Arden Park in Detroit, the home of the Lillian Brooks Coffey Rest Home–a "place apart" for women–with a steering committee of Mary Davis, Jennie L. Hunter, Lucille Jones (Chicago), Tenna Boone (Indiana) and Maydie Payton (New York). Their efforts resulted in the June 1944 purchase of a home from a millionaire, which would be available to "all Christian women." In the *History of the Lillian Brooks Coffey Rest Home*, it is described as a "magnificent old building" featuring unique items such as an organ made in Germany and a bedroom finished in African mahogany.[45]

A Special Commission was established during Mason's declining years and wielded tremendous power over the operations of the Church. Bishop Mason's confidence in the women is seen in a letter written in 1955 with his signature and notarized 1955 appointing Mother Coffey to the Special Commission.[46] The timing of this appointment is significant in that it occurred one week after the last appointment of the men who would lead the church on October 12, 1955, and provides Coffey with the same power alignment.

Coffey Grooms Mother Annie Lee Bailey as National Mother

The year 1919 was a significant one for Blacks on the U.S. East Coast, with Marcus Garvey, the "Black Moses," and his Universal Negro Improvement Association claiming a following of 2,000,000.[47] Another revolution was taking place and Annie Pennington (Bailey) would play a major role. Born September 22, 1894, in Temple, Texas, she was one of nine children of Rev. and Mrs. Felix Garrett. In 1915, when her daughter Clara (from her first marriage) was six years old, she decided to stop by a Holiness revival to "make fun." Upon hearing a testimony of an older woman who was bedridden for five years and had been healed, her heart softened to the message of sanctification and Holy Ghost Baptism. By 1916 she began serving under the leadership of Elder B.J. Mitchell. Three years later she migrated to Buffalo, N.Y., traveling with her pastor, Elder J.E. Bryant, Mother Hattie Robinson Fray, and Mother M.M. Jackson. Joined by Mother Lula Cox of New Jersey and Mother Nancy Gamble of Indiana, the team worked fervently as pioneers establishing the COGIC in New York City; New Jersey; Washington, D.C.; Maryland; Connecticut; Springfield, Mass.; and Boston, and took the ministry to tenement houses, back yards, sheds, and basements.[48] Joseph Paulceus, founder of the first Pentecostal church in Haiti, was a convert of this great evangelist.

Bailey also served as the Masons' governess. Her love was so great for the COGIC founder that after being appointed State Supervisor of Maryland, Delaware, and Washington, D.C., in 1927 and 1928, she vacated her post in 1929 due to his ill health.[49] She married Bishop John Seth Bailey in 1934 and continued to work closely with Coffey as Assistant International Supervisor. When Coffey died in 1964, Bishop O.T. Jones Sr., COGIC's second senior bishop, appointed her third General Supervisor of Women. During her administration, she added many auxiliaries, including the Business and Professional Women's League, National Sunday School Representatives Unit, and revived the women's magazine, *The COGIC Women.*[50]

Premiere Educator Dr. Arenia Mallory

As a result of forced segregation during the early 1900s, Black churches sponsored many normal schools.[51] Mason encouraged the beginning of what was then known as the Saints Home Industrial and Literary School in 1918. Educational pioneer Pinkie Duncan taught classes on mud floors in the basement of Mason's Saint Paul Church in Lexington, with Mason's eldest children and the Cooper children being the first students. The State Board appointed county schoolteacher Professor James Courts of Lexington principal in 1919.

Mason had an unusual knack for discovering women with keen abilities. The women in turn respected their leader and worked untiringly. Understanding the importance of literacy and education to the Church's future, Mason inspired Arenia Mallory to work with disadvantaged students in rural Mississippi. Initially desiring to serve in Africa, she relocated to Lexington and worked with Professor Courts. After her appointment as president, the enrollment opened to all denominations, including Catholics, and the student body rapidly increased from 10 to 350. Mallory compared Mason's belief in her work to that of a father shoring up her resolve despite obstacles. For Mallory, Mason was "[t]he best friend I ever had. He believed in me when I didn't believe in myself. He forgave me as a father for my faults. And *he demanded that men and women give me a chance to build an institution for the church that he gave his life for*. He sent his own children when we didn't have an electric light, nothing but mud. He visited several times a year. In his active years he attended every board meeting."[52]

Mallory's work has been compared to that of her famous colleague and friend Mary McCloud Bethune, who shared her belief that sanctification empowered them for service, love for humanity, and uplifting of the race through education. Butler states, "Their desire to educate the race did not flow simply from their realization that education would improve Black women's condition. Both also felt it was a higher calling, a calling from God."[53] The NAACP's *The Crisis* magazine cites Mallory's having a major role in moving COGIC to the mainstream of Black American church life.[54] A strong personality, her success was in part due to the encouragement of Mason, Coffey, Mother Annie Bailey, and Mother Mattie McGlothen. Mason and the Department of Women were strongly connected to the school, with the Women maintaining it three months of the year. (The Women's Department provided at least $75,000.00 to build and furnish the dining hall.)[55] Because of her close relationship with Bethune, Mallory gained access in many areas, including the Roosevelt White House, where her Jubilee

Harmonizers performed. By 1964 more than 18,000 students would matriculate through Saints,[56] and by 1973 the reported number from across America and foreign countries had increased to 25,000.[57]

Mallory represented COGIC as an educated sanctified leader as member of the National Council of Negro Women (NCNW) U.S., International Council of Women ; a 1954 delegate of National Council of Women (NCW) in Helsinki and special guest of the Swedish Council; a 1956 Vice President of NCW of the U.S.; and Mother's Day Speaker at the Dexter Avenue Baptist Church on October 14, 1956.[58] In 1959 she was among the "women leaders of the free world" who participated in the policy-making program of the International Council of Women Executive Board meeting in Vienna, Austria. At Istanbul, she was elected Vice Governor of the Educational Commission of the International Council of Women.[59] The news of her work spread across the country and the Department of Labor's Bureau of Manpower, Automation, and Training tapped her to serve as a Manpower Development Specialist in the interest of deprived and disadvantaged people.

The success in utilizing the Church's resources to its full extent could be felt across the nation. The frame of empowerment was intrinsic within the fabric of the Church, and women, with the long view of establishing sound legacies that would transcend generations, used powerful language to shape their ministries. In 1929 the twenty-six-year-old Cora Agnes Berry (1903–1976) became sanctified and immediately began working at the Belsuever COGIC in Los Angeles. She conducted revivals and tent services, purchased a church (which she gave over to Elder P.L. Lockett), and worked out a mission (which she gave to Elder Leonard Jones). She urged others to take advantage of the power women held within the COGIC:

> Now is the time...to assume your rightful place in the world. Within the realm of your own mind, you have exalted powers, which you should put to actual, practical, immediate use. Realize the GREAT MENTAL RESOURCES at your ready command, and resolve to make better and larger use of your daily opportunities. Get a clear mental picture of what you ought to do, then keep it before you as a constant inspiration. There is an inexhaustible field open for your talents and energies. All things necessary are yours IF YOU BUT TAKE THEM.[60]

A product of Saints[61] and Los Angeles State College, the former public school teacher used her gifts as the Dean of the Emmanuel Institute, whose mission was "born of the need to perpetuate the gospel…and produce informed, Pentecostal…witnesses…who can tell the wonderful story of Jesus equally as well in industrial and business centers as in places of worship."[62] When Mother Coffey expanded the WIC to include a leadership conference, Berry was appointed to the team and later became Director. The late Supervisor Odessa Newman stated, "In 1951…Mother Coffey projected the Leadership Conference and Mother Berry implemented the idea."[63] Berry also served as Vice President of the National Board of Education and board member of Mason Theological Seminary. In December 1973, Dr. A.C. Mallory conferred upon her an honorary doctorate.

MASON INSPIRES FEMALE MISSIONARIES AND EVANGELISTS

As Mason watched God fulfill His promise, he understood that the women, who organized, prayed, evangelized, sang, and worked untiringly, assisted in its fulfillment. Seeing the need for the training of young children, Mason organized the Sunshine Band in 1911 with Mother Lydia Hinsley appointed the first "Big Sister Sunshine." By 1949, long before federal Head Start programs, Hinsley organized a nursery that cared for children of working mothers. She stated, "I saw that the children in these vital years were in real need of some type of training. Nothing was being done."[64] She opened the nursery at Hinsley Cathedral COGIC where her husband was pastor.

Bishop Mason's support of women's ministries had a profound effect upon thousands of women. According to Mother Lillian Brooks Coffey, "[D]areless women…followed their chief apostle. Like the women of old we have laid at his feet. We know his teachings. Bishop Mason loved the women. He didn't only spend his time with the men of this church. But he spent much time, much time, with his daughters. He was kind to us. We followed him over this country and sang the songs of Zion. We took down our beds out of our living rooms and let him come in and establish the church from coast to coast. We have a part of this ministry."[65] He was known for his power with God which could be attributed to his well-known prayer vigils. It is telling that he wished for his sons and his daughters to take on the mantle of prayer to keep their souls athirst and the life of the church robust. Mother Eula Dabney, known for her stamina in praying through great obstacles, was encouraged to continue her prayer ministry by the apostle. The date of birth of Elizabeth Juanita (Eula) Dabney is unknown, but she often said she learned the value of prayer from her mother, who always kept a family altar in their home.[66] In her classical book, *What It Means to Pray Through*, she tells the story of when Mason personally met with her to assure her of his defense of her ministry:

> I told the Lord if He sent Bishop Mason before the week closed, I would be confident and satisfied to work for Him, regardless of what the future presented. The next morning, at ten o'clock, Bishop Mason called; he was at the Pennsylvania Station in Washington, D.C., enroute to the Pittsburgh Conference. The pastor rushed to the station, and related to him how God had supplied spiritual bread to the city... Bishop Mason prayed...and sent him back with a message for me to "Keep on Praying; the outpour would be greater." In fourteen days the Lord saved ninety-five souls. Late one night, a telephone call came from Pastor Carr stating Bishop Mason wanted me to meet him in Baltimore the next afternoon. The devil told me that Bishop Mason wanted to rebuke me as others had done... When we arrived...I was so weak...they had to lead me...where Bishop Mason was waiting... After Elder Dabney related the story...[Mason] drew near unto me and took my hand, and the Lord led him out in prayer. Then he read the Scripture: "yea everyone who lives godly in Christ Jesus shall suffer persecution." He told me not to pay any attention to the devil and his attacks, but to press forward; God had greatly overshadowed and blessed me with the spirit of prayer, *like unto his ministry. He told me it was his long, long prayer request answered.* [*Emphasis added*][67]

Women like Dabney, confident of the blessings of their leader, were undaunted as they pushed back against those within their ranks who did not share their vision and attempted to jeopardize or hinder the great work God was doing through their lives. She revealed, "As time passed on, they tried to contaminate Bishop Mason's mind with these same evil thoughts, but he rebuked them sharply for their carnal minds, and unbelief in God."[68]

Bishop Mason was also known for spiritual songs given to him by God. Early in her life the powerful Evangelist Emily Bibby, who later served as assistant pastor to General Board Member Bishop F.D. Washington, was honored to serve him. She recounted, "I used to play for Dad Mason sometimes. When the Spirit of the Lord gave him songs, I could catch him anywhere. When others couldn't play for him, I could. I don't know how I did it, but it was a blessing from God."[69]

Mother Ola Mae Haynes was appointed the first Chairman of Burner's for Africa, which supported missions in Africa, with Mother Larry Fields as National Co-chairman, who felt her ministry was appointed by God and approved by her leaders. In the 32nd WIC held in Detroit, then 85-year-old Fields writes of her salvation experience, assisting in praying out (planting) a church in cotton fields:

> They wouldn't let us in the school house, but we nailed a nail on a shade tree and hung up a brass coal oil lamp for light at night. The Lord saved the schoolteacher and she opened up the schoolhouse. There is an old established Church of God in Christ there today. After I moved to California, under Bishop S.M. Crouch and Mother L.O. Hale we helped to pray out 10 churches and worked [to] help pay rent… I was trained to work with my hands and help the church, and to stretch forth my hands to the need by Dad Mason, Mother Lillian B. Coffey, St. Samuel, and Mother Anna Piles.[70]

A young O.T. Jones Sr. journeyed to Oklahoma, where he met John Morris, a former Baptist minister who received the Baptism of the Holy Ghost and established the first Pentecostal church near Enid. His twin daughters Leatha and Reatha, born in 1900, proved to be extraordinary evangelists. Announced as "Misses Reatha and Leatha Morris, The Evangelist Twins" the women sang, played instruments, were used by God to perform miracles of healing and deliverance, and "prayed out" up to 100 churches in the COGIC. The following offers a glimpse how Mason's delegation to Mother Robinson empowered women to spread the gospel:

> My poppa invited [O.T. Jones] in and…I heard him tellin' momma and poppa about [the] the Church of God in Christ… [T]hat… Bishop Charles Harrison Mason…a great leader…was inviting everyone to Memphis. When Leatha and I got there, we saw hundreds of Negro people…preaching and teaching day and night. This was our first "Church of God in Christ" experience. Mr. O.T. Jones…told Bishop Mason and a woman named Lizzie Robinson

> about us. Not long after...she quickly gave us a letter of recommendation...[and] put us right to work!...She sent us to...help preachers... Some churches started on front porches, backyards, or even in the living rooms of houses... *She just gave us orders[emphasis added] and we followed them.*[71]

Mother Fannie Page of Eastern Tennessee wrote, "I have witnessed the sick healed, the sight of the blind restored, the lame leaping and praised God; people leaving wheel chairs in the church going home healed...all through the prayers of this righteous man...an instrument in the hands of Almighty God [he] prayed death off my body in 1939."[72] Annie Lee Stamps was called at the age of seven "by a sweet voice calling her name." She was healed by God's power through Bishop Mason. After she accepted the evangelist call, she was tutored in the work by the apostle himself and wrote: "What a blessing to be riding on the train with Bishop Mason. I had been sick four years and could eat...only liquids in 1926. Bishop Mason prayed for me in 1934. The next morning I ate all solid foods... Desiring to know the secret of God's miracle power in this great leader...I asked questions. He answered: 'It is the Gift of Faith, with much suffering to follow.'"[73] That foundational mentoring came in handy as Stamps truly began to suffer. Because she had observed the unwavering faith of Bishop Mason, she says she "waited on God... I was reaching for the Gift of Faith."[74] Bishop Mason's great gift of faith could have led to him allowing those in awe of his healing power to surround him with a cult of personality. It is interesting to note that he projected these gifts away from himself and upwards toward God. While it would be presumptuous or foolish to offer a Pollyanna portrayal of early COGIC leaders, the sanctified women of COGIC history exhibited a sense of fellowship and camaraderie in moving forward toward common goals. During Mason's travels in the Jim Crow South era, Elder S.M. Boyd and his wife Colorado State Supervisor Boyd welcomed him into their home. She was miraculously healed of a bad heart and a spot on her lungs, recalling, "In May 1926, I went into his room one morning, as was my custom, to help him and see if he needed a clean shirt or socks. This morning...Dad Mason looked at me and said, "Death, the Lord rebuke you!"[75]

The work expanded globally and courageous women helped spread the fire of the Holy Ghost. Prior to President Dwight Eisenhower officially signing legislature to make Alaska statehood official

(1959), "In 1947 a saintly woman, Mother Josephine Stephens... influenced by the Power of the Holy Ghost...and her sister began their first Prayer and Bible Band, which was the beginning of the Church of God in Christ in the [eventual] State of Alaska."[76] Mary McClahlin started the COGIC in her home in 1948, thus making the COGIC England's first Black church.[77] Her daughter, current England Supervisor of Women Mary Reynolds, recalled observing Mason at the World Pentecostal Conference held in England in 1951 or 1952:

> I remember Donald McGee [saying], 'This is Bishop Mason of the Church of God in Christ.' [McGee] told us about Azusa and that Bishop Mason is lovingly known as Dad. It was a joy to see the room full of White ministers on the platform stand to attention...and never sat down until Dad Mason finished! He blessed everybody and when he returned to his seat, they sat down. I have never, ever seen it happen anywhere else. I was very proud to be Black...because there were only a few of us in the congregation. [It was] an honor to God.[78]

COGIC's First Female International Missionaries

In a sense Mason legitimized their work by giving them equal power and opportunity outside the proscribed societal boundaries in the field of foreign missions. Under Mason's leadership COGIC female representatives established missions in Jamaica (1919), Turks and Caicos Islands (1922), Haiti (1929), and Canada (1920s).[79] While in Europe or America they would be limited largely to domestic duties, in these locations COGIC women preached, taught, and practiced medicine. Lillian Brooks Coffey noted their earliest forays: "The foreign work of this church was not pioneered by men, it was pioneered and fostered and is being carried on actively by women of this great church."[80] In 1939 Beatrice Lott, a young Texan surrendering to the call, made the first of at least fourteen journeys to Liberia for "fighting the practice of witchcraft and devil doctors, who often tormented young believers."[81] In 1944 *The Progressive Youth* Editor, Elder S.A. Jordan, reported Lott and Martha Barber arrived safely in Cape Palmas, Liberia. The report also provided details on their furlough activities, during which Lott "traveled through the state lecturing [and] told of her ministerial, mechanical and engineering experiences, building houses, churches, highways and bridges. She told how she stood on the banks of the river and announced the ceremony while the natives immersed the baptismal candidates into the water and how she stood at the grave and pronounced the ritual while the dead was laid to rest."[82]

Between 1947 and 1952 Liberian pioneer Elizabeth White, along with Francena Wiggins, had grown the Manula Station to a membership of 50, supported a day school, began the mission buildings, organized the church, brought new churches in, and operated a full mission program. A 1952 souvenir journal reported they operated an elementary school where "present enrollment is 45 [with] 15 boarding students, outdoor clinic, established and received a church about ten miles from [their station] and carried several evangelistic services to every surrounding town within fifteen miles of our station [oftentimes] staying overnight…among the heathens that they might hear the gospel."[83]

CONCLUSION

In studying Mason's approach to women's ministries, it is important to consider that he was a visionary, which, by definition, would have him view roles and structures of the patriarchy in a new way. It should be evident that Mason's leadership style (legitimizing the import of their work in giving women equal power and opportunity) bypassed conventional patriarchal wisdom (in his assignments to women), succeeding in bridging dichotomous societal beliefs and values and allowing him to use those women who availed themselves to leadership. Thus, he also transformed the male leadership vision to include the talents of the women. In allowing them great freedom to serve the Lord, his ability to influence scores of women to perform daunting tasks is a testament to the genius of following God's lead in organizational and cultural change. Bishop Mason, his followers, and the sanctified women achieved great victories in the cause of Christ during the early twentieth century! Many women, such as Lizzie Robinson, Lillian Brooks Coffey, Dr. Arenia Mallory, and so many others influenced by the founder of COGIC, performed amazing feats that enlarged the territory of the denomination. Bishop C.H. Mason built a kind of ecosystem in which the ideas, goals, and desires of the organization's female constituents could grow and flourish. It if weren't for Mason's genius of developing strategic alliances through a strong women's department, COGIC may not have been the paradigmatic organization it is today.

7

SEEKING THE JUST SOCIETY

Charles Harrison Mason's Quest for Social Equality

RAYNARD D. SMITH

INTRODUCTION

In their classic sociological study, *The Black Church in the African American Experience*, C. Eric Lincoln and Lawrence Mamiya identify a pattern within Black churches in which they see a vacillation between priestly functions in which they attend to the spiritual needs of their constituents and the prophetic functions in which they assert themselves as social critiques of society.[1] As opposed to other social scientists who viewed either one or the other, Lincoln and Mamiya see Black churches operating in a dialectical tension on a continuum between these two functions, the priestly and prophetic, in response to historical times. This essay is an attempt to situate Charles Harrison Mason and the Church of God in Christ within this continuum of the priestly and prophetic in seeking to explore Mason's moral vision in response to the issue of racism in America. The questions guiding this research are: What types of strategies did Mason employ addressing the problem of racism? To what moral norms did he subscribe? What are the limits of his moral view? How are these claims grounded? And, lastly, what community is he addressing? As a black preacher seeking to achieve human fulfillment and the just society, I contend that Mason embodied both the priestly function in which he advocated prayer and "supplication" *and* the prophetic in which he called for social resistance.[2] First, I will briefly set Mason within his historical and socio-political context.

MASON'S SOCIO-POLITICAL CONTEXT

When Mason began his ministry in 1893 in Preston, Arkansas, the U.S. was a hostile place for people of African descent. In 1865 slavery of people of African ancestry was abolished. after this came the passage of the Civil Rights Act of 1867, extending enfranchisement to the newly freed people as America embarked on a new course in terms of race relations. People of African ancestry entered the political process with the intent of creating a just and moral social order for Blacks as well as Whites. August Meier characterizes the decade of this period of Reconstruction (1867–1877) as a time of great optimism.[3] However, this period of euphoria was short-lived. With the Compromise of 1877 under the administration of President Hayes, the social, political, and economic gains made by African Americans witnessed a precipitous decline. Vindictive Southern White conservatives and radicals regained control of local, state, and federal legislatures. Besides using chicanery and mob violence, they set about disfranchising African Americans through such means as poll taxes, good conduct clauses, grandfather clauses, and proof of literacy clauses.[4] Systematic programs of legally separating Whites and people of African ancestry on the basis of race on every level of society were instituted. This process of exclusion and subordination achieved full status in 1896 with the Supreme Court ruling of Plessy vs. Ferguson sanctioning the "separate but equal" doctrine as the law of the land.[5] This doctrine solidified the fate of African Americans to second-class citizenship. Lynching became a prevalent form of violence used to enforce the social mores of White supremacy, with more than 2500 known cases occurring between 1884–1900.[6] Historian Rayford Logan characterized the period from 1877–1901 as the "nadir" in the life of African Americans.[7] This was the socio-political context that shaped and informed Mason's psyche and ministry.

THE IMPACT OF SLAVE RELIGION

Mason's quest for human fulfillment and the moral good was directly influenced by his socio-political reality. In response to the societal oppression he encountered, Mason sought the comforts of his religion to find meaning and order. This religion that brought meaning and coherence was slave religion. Born in 1864[8] to former slaves, Jerry (Jeremiah) and Eliza (Nelson) Mason, on the outskirts of Memphis, Tennessee, Mason was exposed to the rich cultural and religious heritage of his forbears. His parents were religious people steeped in the Afro-Baptist religious tradition. Mason's mother, being a very devout woman given to prayer, especially saw to it that the religious practices of the slave religion were inculcated in young Mason and his siblings.

In regards to the nature of this religion, historian Mechal Sobel has argued that the African sacred cosmos that existed on the shores of West Africa underwent a radical transformation when it came into contact with Western religion (Christianity) and the reality of the institution of slavery.[9] Although Blacks were converted to Christianity early in their history in America, it was not until the Great Awakening, with its emphasis on emotionally expressive religious experience rather than rational assent to doctrine, that people of African descent began to accept Christianity in large numbers. What emerged from this experience was a new sacred cosmos by which people of African ancestry could interpret the vicissitudes of life as a slave in America. African American historian Albert Raboteau asserts, "Africans and their descendants in Protestant America discovered analogues in revivalistic evangelicalism to the religious beliefs and rituals of Africa. These analogues turned out to be crucial for the process of reinterpretation that made Christianity intelligible and adaptable for large numbers of African Americans."[10] From within the sacred canopy of slave religion, expressive forms of worship such as trances, dreams, visions, and the ring shout were normative religious behaviors and therefore socially acceptable and expected. Most important, this helped to give coherence and meaning to Black life. Sobel contends, "The internalization of this sacred cosmos is the crucial aspect of an individual's socialization and of his [sic] life. Through the internalization of a coherent sacred cosmos, the potentially chaotic and frightening infinity of events 'fall in place,' and the life of the individual assumes purpose and direction. The individual is given categories of meaning, ways of looking at and evaluating reality, an 'inner hierarchy of significance.'"[11]

The sacred canopy of slave religion impacted and infused Mason's perspective on his existential socio-political reality and the reality of most people of African ancestry. Furthermore, I contend that it affected and informed his leadership and the strategies he employed in addressing the issue of race relations in the segregated South. In their desire to seek relief from their oppressive conditions, the slaves sought the comfort of their religion. Slave religion provided African Americans with the ability to interpret their world events from a liberationist perspective. Theologian James Evans has argued that African Americans read the Bible with "new eyes" that were informed by their lived reality of oppression and their inner longing for liberation from the oppressive forces.[12] He contends:

> The Exodus experience was an archetypal myth that, while drawn from Scripture, became the lens through which the Bible was read… The Exodus account reflected in a striking way the experience of the slaves. It required no stretch of the imagination to see the trials of the Israelites as paralleling the trials of the slaves, Pharaoh and his army as oppressors, and Egyptland as the South.[13]

A predominant motif that emerged from their reading of the Exodus event was God as liberator. They had witnessed God's liberating action in their lives when, as they interpreted it, God used President Abraham Lincoln and the Union soldiers to destroy the yoke of slavery.[14]

MASON'S MORAL VISION

Mason's moral vision was no less influenced by this liberation hermeneutic. Mason, too, saw parallels between the Exodus narrative and the experience of African Americans in the segregated South. Deeply rooted within the sacred cosmos of slave religion, Mason believed that just as it took divine intervention to destroy the institution of slavery, it would require this same intervention to resolve the problem of racial injustice perpetrated against people of African ancestry.[15] However, it was not that Mason had come to accept the purported doctrine that Blacks were inherently inferior to Whites. On the contrary, he firmly believed in social equality. Yet, it appears that Mason recognized the sensitive nature that surrounded the race issue in the South. He was aware of its ability to incite White hostility, leading to senseless violence and bloodshed that was usually at the expense of African Americans. For this cause Mason advocated conciliation and gradualism in his approach to the race problem in the South. Through persistent prayer, patience, and humility Mason believed God would effect a change in which a just and moral society would be established in which African Americans would experience true equality.[16] During the early days of his ministry as a Holiness minister affiliated with C.P. Jones, the denominational paper *Truth*, ran a leading article entitled, "A Message of Hope for the Black Man: How He May Get Thro [sic] This

Awful Time," which strongly reflects Mason's position of humility and prayer:

> O black man, that is thine only door. Proudly despise it if thou wilt, but one wiser than all of us has said, that pride goes before destruction and a haughty spirit before a fall... God resists the proud, but gives grace (shows favor) to the humble. All under hold is better in a wrestling match than all top hold. A cave in a hillside is better than a tree top in a storm. Few men [sic] are knocked down from their knees. The little dog assuming a humble air keeps the big dog off. The man [sic] on the ground cannot fall from the pinnacle. The meek way is the gospel way. The knee way is the sure way.[17]

The article continues in its admonishing tone, advocating a passive position in terms of resolving the race problem. African Americans are encouraged to endure the hardship of racial oppression without any retaliation and to persist in prayer as opposed to agitating for social justice:

> We must not tire in prayer. We must groan and bear, grin and endure, love our enemies, bless them that curse us, do good to them that hate us, make the best of everything and be all the while looking to God... The colored people need to do this that [sic] now, neither ought there be delay. Nineveh did it. Are we better than they?... O if our leaders would humbly consider this! We could then change sentiment in America. God would do it.[18]

Social ethicist Peter Paris identifies this strategy as pastoral, noting that its main function was to provide comfort to the downtrodden while instilling hope in those who were on the brink of despair. It considered the dismal socio-political reality of African Americans, pointed to a transcendent source of strength and help while yet offering a critique of the injustices of the segregated South.[19]

Another aspect of Mason's moral vision derived from the African American sacred cosmos is what Paris calls the principle of "nonracism"–which is derived from the theological supposition of the common humanity of all people.[20] Mason's understanding of his faith was integrally tied to the Bible. His explication of the faith was devoid of any scientific or philosophical categories by which to establish the truth of the biblical message. His fundamental presupposition was that the Bible record of the story of Jesus as told in the Gospels and explained in the Epistles was wholly true. The Bible was the source and ground of truth and the basis for what was just and good. With the Bible as his supreme guide for faith and practice, Mason believed that "out of one blood was made many nations."[21] Therefore, for Mason, social equality was a universal right ordained by God. If one breached this right one would be in direct violation of God's law and therefore subject to bringing down upon oneself divine retribution.

Throughout his preaching career as well as during the founding and development of his denomination,[22] the Church of God in Christ (COGIC), Mason sought to embody the ethical teaching that emphasized the common humanity of all people. In his attempt to live true to this principle, he defied the social norms of the segregated South. In a time of Jim Crow laws when it was unlawful for Blacks and Whites to assemble together, Mason was often known to fellowship with Whites. He often traveled throughout the South with a White COGIC minister, William B. Holt, to preach.[23] He accepted invitations to preach to White congregations. Mason stated, "In the Spring of 1916 I was invited by the authorities of the city of Nashville, Tenn., to hold camp meeting for the white people. The city auditorium, with a seating capacity of 7,000, was furnished and equipped by the citizens of the city... Many of the best white people of the city attended the meeting. The Holy Spirit through me did wonderful things."[24] Of another occasion his biographer writes, "Another call for the whites, by C.M. Grace of Little Rock, Ark., in the year 1919 in the tabernacle in Little Rock with seating capacity 7,000 or more, God so wonderfully wrought His power among both white and black sanctifying, baptizing and healing."[25] Moreover, as founder and leader of his own organization, Mason welcomed Whites as equal partners in ministry.[26] In 1925, Holt, mentioned above, who was Mason's traveling companion and a White man, became the General Secretary of the denomination and was later appointed by Mason to serve as Overseer of the state of Washington in 1927.[27] Mason also cooperated with other White Pentecostals such as Howard Goss, Mack Pinson, H.G. Rodgers, and Leonard Adams, allowing them to use his COGIC charter as a covering for their ministerial credentialing to perform marriages and qualify for reduced rates on the railroad.[28] In 1914 when some members of this group of White clergy chose to formalize their own denomination, the Assemblies of God, Mason, although not formally invited, attended the organizational meeting, preached a sermon, and bid them God's speed.[29] Even after the separation of a large number of Whites from the COGIC, Mason's denomination continued to welcome Whites. In 1924 a White conference consisting of the White congregations within the COGIC was created.[30] This lead to the organizational development of the White Churches of God in Christ headquartered at Woodworth-Etter Tabernacle under the jurisdiction of August Feick, general superintendent and pastor of the tabernacle in Indianapolis, Indiana.[31]

COGIC historian David Daniels asserts, "This development was in response to the argument of the white clergy who accepted the anomaly of white congregations in black denominations and being a racial minority with the larger system, yet sought to maximize their presence by uniting under a white administrative unit."[32] Since these events occurred during the time of strict segregation, how does one account for Mason's actions? I contend the answer can be found in Mason's introduction to and involvement with William J. Seymour and the Azusa Street Revival. In 1906 Mason's longing for a deeper life was stirred with news that a revival had started in Los Angeles in which a recently rediscovered religious experience–the Baptism of the Holy Spirit–was being received by believers. This revival was being conducted by an African American preacher, William J. Seymour, in an abandoned livery stable on Azusa Street. Mason decided that he must go to Los Angeles to investigate this new phenomenon. Accompanying him were two other COGIC ministers, David J. Young and John A. Jeter. At the Azusa Street Revival, Mason witnessed people of various races and nationalities worshiping God together in harmony and equality. In the words of Frank Bartleman, at Azusa, Mason experienced that the "color line was washed away by the blood."[33] The Azusa Street Revival played a pivotal role in Mason's life, for it wedded the experience of his slave religion and the ethical principle of the common family of humanity with the experience of Spirit Baptism. This experience would later have a profound influence on Mason's moral vision of a racially inclusive community. COGIC historian Ithiel Clemmons contends,

> It was C.H. Mason...who grasped and stood with Seymour in the revival that united glossolalia with the Pauline vision of an

> all-inclusive egalitarian fellowship in which there is "...neither Jew nor Greek, bond nor free,...male nor female..."(Galatians 3:28, Colossians 3:11).[34]

However, despite Mason's best intentions to adhere to the racially inclusive and egalitarian vision that he had encountered at the Azusa Street Revival, his efforts were doomed to failure. The societal pressures to conform to the social customs and conventions of American society would prove too great a social force to challenge and prevail. In the mid 1930s the separate body, the White Churches of God in Christ, with denominational headquarters in Indianapolis, Indiana, had been dissolved.[35] Daniels states, "The white conference existed until the early 1930s when the predominantly black leadership abolished the conference, accusing the white leadership of attempting to form a white separate denomination out of the COGIC."[36] With the withdrawal of the White clergy, thus ended the racially inclusive community Mason envisioned and sought to achieve.

MASON SPEAKING OUT AGAINST SOCIAL/RACIAL INJUSTICE

In addition to Mason defying the racial social order of his time through actions, he also spoke out against the injustices that African Americans encountered at the hands of Whites. Mason was known to have clear ideas about segregation. James Delk, a member of Mason's denomination since 1904, writes of Mason, "I am a white man and Brother Mason a colored man. But bear in mind that neither Brother Mason nor myself believe in segregation or Jim Crow but all people, either white or colored, do not see this in the same light that brother Mason and myself see it."[37] Delk's reflection about Mason suggests that Mason held clear views concerning the issue of racism in America. Mason never internalized the norms of the segregated society. In fact, in his sermons and actions Mason attacked the social injustices of segregation. Known for his oratorical and charismatic abilities, Mason drew crowds upward of two to three thousand people as he canvassed the South as an itinerant Holiness evangelist and later as Overseer of his denomination. He often used these occasions to comment on race relations in America. As mentioned earlier, it was a common characteristic for the ex-slaves to see God moving in nature and history. Mason, too, shared this worldview. In a sermon entitled "Storms," Mason asserted:

> Some of the wise of today are saying that God has nothing to do with storm [sic]. But the Bible says: "the Lord will have His way in the whirlwinds and in the storms."...In a little town, De Soto, where there was much race hatred, I am told that a sign, bearing these words was raised, "Negroes: read and run." God performed another one of His strange acts. This town was completely destroyed.[38]

This sermon preached in the mid 1920s is a clear example of how Mason viewed God in relation to the issue of racial oppression in America. Mason understood the destruction of the town of De Soto noted for its racial hatred as a pronouncement of God's judgment and wrath, which were in direct response to De Soto's oppression of African Americans. Clearly this was Mason's way of critiquing the injustices that existed in society. For Mason, racism was a sin that only God could resolve, and he believed that God would. Yet, Mason's critique also functioned to instill hope in those who were the oppressed in that it located God on their side in their struggle to achieve human dignity and fulfillment. In addition, for Mason, God moved in the storms to demonstrate to White society God's divine ordering of the races. Mason believed African Americans were not created to be segregated nor subjugated to Whites but instead to be socially equal. Mason states, "In a Mississippi storm a colored child was carried by the storm and placed in a white man's yard."[39] Mason's identification of the distinct racial groups, "colored" and "white," coupled with the use of nature, the storm, suggests that Mason believed God's divine plan was for Blacks and Whites to live together in social harmony. There was no doubt in Mason's mind that the God who had created all people from one blood also created the races to coexist in a mutually affirming relationship. At the Azusa Street Revival, Mason witnessed this fact first hand. Blacks, Whites, Latinos, and Asians came together to receive the blessing of Spirit Baptism. Nowhere does this message come across clearer than in Bishop Louis Ford's reflections on Mason teachings. Ford, a convert to COGIC in his youth, educated at the denominational school Saints Academy in Lexington,

Mississippi, and later elevated to the position of Presiding Bishop, asserted that Mason drew upon the principles of natural theology to argue for the proper social relationship of Blacks and Whites. Here, he notes how Mason used the construction of the eye as an analogy to explain how God had set the races in divine order to coexist in harmony. He states:

> Mason would often say, "Ah, here in my eyes is the darkie, you may call it the blackie. And there's the whitey in there. Now, if you destroy the whitey, the blackie can't see because it holds the blackie together. And if you destroy the blackie, which is the sight, the whitey can't see. God is giving us a message that we must work together as one.[40]

Yes, Mason envisioned a just society in which Blacks and Whites lived, worked, and worshiped together. For Mason this was not seen as wishful thinking but biblically and theologically supported and confirmed in the coming of the Spirit. If through the principle of nonracism Mason believed in the equality of the races, with the coming of the Baptism of the Holy Spirit he envisioned one was endued with power to transform society.[41]

In addition, so confident in his belief that racism was not acceptable, Mason sought to challenge the social norm by calling for his COGIC constituents throughout the country to boycott the buses that offered inadequate service and treatment to Blacks.. In 1931 through a special announcement published in his denominational paper, *The Whole Truth*, in an article entitled, "An Appeal to Ride the Railroads," Mason expressed his disfavor with the way in which African Americans were receiving inferior treatment from the bus lines both in terms of employing African Americans and creating comfortable conditions. The announcement in the paper challenged the moral sensibilities of his constituents, "Now have you seen one colored driver on any of your great bus lines? No." It continues encouraging them to patronize the trains, "When you ride the trains you are helping to keep *your own* in work… They employ thousands of *our people*…[and] they also give us a better consideration."[42] Thus, on the prospects or receiving better treatment and employment opportunities, i.e., having a record of treating African Americans with greater respect and dignity, Mason vehemently recommended that his constituents patronize the trains over the buses when coming to the national meetings.

MASON'S OPPOSITION TO WORLD WAR I

Perhaps the greatest challenge to Mason's quest for the just society occurred during World War I. It appears that Mason had an irrevocable determination to share in the American dream. He viewed African Americans as part and parcel of the American body politic. Nowhere is this ambiguity more evident than in his sermon preached in 1918 entitled, "The Kaiser in the Light of the Scriptures." In this sermon, Mason sanctioned supporting America's wartime efforts by encouraging COGIC members to purchase war bonds. He asserted, "Our government is asking us for a loan, as we are in no violation of God's word in granting it."[43] However, with the coming of World War I, Mason's allegiance to America, to God, and to his race were put to the test. In March 1917, when the United States declared war on Germany and its allies, it was thought the key to victory was military might in massive numbers. With this goal in mind, three months later all able bodied men between the ages of twenty-one and thirty-one were required to register for the draft. Only those with justifiable causes would be exempt. With patriotism at an all-time high, it was bordering on sedition to speak against the war efforts. However, because of his religious beliefs, Mason encouraged his male parishioners to seek exemption claiming conscientious objection. Undergirding this decision was the fact that Mason firmly believed that the Bible taught against the taking of any human life. His church's doctrinal statement reflected this belief: "We believe the shedding of human blood or taking of human life to be contrary to the teachings of our Lord and Savior, and as a body, we are averse to war in all its various forms."[44] Yet, besides the doctrinal position of the denomination Mason also held deep personal convictions against African Americans enlisting in the war. Mason had witnessed how Whites were vehemently opposed to African Americans wearing their military uniforms in America.[45] Thus, Mason questioned the legitimacy of African Americans fighting for democracy abroad when they had no democracy at home.[46]

It appears that Mason's denominational position coupled with his personal critique of America's treatment of African American citizens proved so persuasive that in Holmes County, Mississippi, where Mason's church was located and the population nearly 80 percent Black, more than half of those eligible for the draft failed to report for duty.[47] For his convictions and the fact that Mason's church was "known" to associate with "strange men of German extraction" Mason eventually came under surveillance of the government. White citizens of Holmes County alleged that Mason was sowing seeds of subversion in his sermons by discouraging African Americans from enlisting in the war efforts.[48] With White antipathy rising, he was jailed in Lexington for obstruction of the draft.[49] Not too long after that, Mason was also jailed in Paris, Texas, on similar charges.[50] Yet Mason refused to recant his denomination's position even amid the growing pressure exerted by the federal government seeking to indict him for sedition.

In October 1918, when the grand jury met in Texas, Mason and his followers were exonerated. Theodore Kornweibel suggests that news of the imminent defeat of the Germans, and thus the end of the war, may have influenced the outcome of the grand jury's proceedings.[51] However, Mason would later reminisce and interpret it as this: "The enemy (the devil) tried to hinder me and bound me over in jail for several days. I thank God for the persecution. 'For all that will live Godly must suffer persecution.'"[52] For Mason, to live Godly was to assert one's right to be here and be in equal relationship with all people. The controversy was over. Mason had spoken out against America's sin of racism, and for this he encountered hardship and distress. Yet Mason held firm to his conviction and in doing this he witnessed God's righteousness prevail. It seemed that Mason emerged the victor faithful to God, faithful to his race, and faithful to his country.

CONCLUSION

In conclusion, Mason was a man of his times who, in his quest for justice and human fulfillment at a time when race relations were disparagingly low, sought in his pastoral function to discern the will of God for America in terms of race relations. True to his priestly/pastoral function, he sought to protect those African Americans whom God had entrusted to his care, yet, he did not polarize Blacks and Whites leaving little latitude for reconciliation. He never gave up hope, but was always looking forward to the day that God would bring about social equality. Known for his life of dedication and prayer, Mason would supplicate, "A better day Lord, a better day."[53] Mason's quest for the just society is a testimony of his faith. This faith was expressed through the sacred canopy of slave religion and the Azusa Street vision of a racially egalitarian community in a God who liberates, sustains, empowers, and who is "no respecter of persons."

8

"A More Excellent Way"

The Theological Journey of Bishop Charles Harrison Mason in the Theological Formation of the Church of God in Christ

David D. Daniels III

Introduction

Theology profoundly shaped the life and ministry of Bishop Charles Harrison Mason. His theological journey left an indelible imprint on the doctrine of the Church of God in Christ and paved a theological trajectory within North American Pentecostalism that has had an immense impact on the Black Church throughout the twentieth century. Mason could be classified as a folk or organic theologian. Folk theologians communicate the Christian faith in "plain words for plain people" by engaging in a theological reflection that is "practical and occasional" rather than theoretical and systematic. They draw from the language of prayer, praise, song, sermons, testimonies, and exhortation as well as the vocabulary of everyday life. While their focus is not upon theological method and dialogues with philosophy, their theologies bring Scripture as the cardinal theological source that bears on the dilemmas that structure the Christian life and community.[1]

Along Mason's theological journey, he engaged in debates, endured controversies, learned new positions, and arrived at destinations. His theological journey formed him and shaped the doctrinal statements that COGIC crafted. These doctrinal statements bear the marks of Mason's journey: choosing sides in the debates, responding to the controversies, echoing syntheses, and reflecting consensus. Consequently, COGIC's doctrinal statements are best interpreted within the theological milieu through which Mason traveled, providing the cues and context by which to hear the statements.

In this essay I will argue that Mason's theological journey through the African American strands of Baptist, Restorationist, Holiness, and Pentecostal thought shaped the crafting of COGIC doctrinal statements, making COGIC theology more a product of the African American Protestant theological traditions than a mere recycling of Wesleyan or Keswick theologies. Grounded within Afro-Pentecostal studies, this inquiry will draw upon Black theological studies represented by the scholarship of James H. Cone, Peter Paris, and Cheryl Sanders, and upon Pentecostal theological studies represented by the scholarship of Leonard Lovett, Donald Dayton, Frank Macchia, and Douglas Jacobsen.[2]

EMBARKING ON A THEOLOGICAL JOURNEY: THE HOLINESS QUEST

The quest for holiness inspired Mason's theological journey. During the first half of his life, holiness seized his imagination; he envisioned Christians living the holy life consistently. As a youth, he pondered the contrast between those different ecclesial communities marked by holiness and those that were less so. In an early biographical account, Mason reflected on the difference between the birthplace and homestead of his childhood, which was marked by Christian qualities, and the ungodly environment into which his family relocated during his adolescence. His homestead was informed by "a religion like that he heard the old folks talk about and manifest in their lives," in which there exists a correspondence between the teaching and practice of the Christian faith, the Christian testimony, and lifestyle. Mason's theological journey reflected his desire "to return to the old homestead."[3]

Theologically, the dilemma that Mason confronted in the church concerning the low moral status of the laity and the clergy was how to interpret justification. The popular understanding of justification by Baptists during Mason's early years was that justification as an act of God became irrevocable and unrelated to the Christian behavior, even immoral behavior; as God's act, justification remained secure for Christians in spite of their constant sinning. During Mason's early years, the low moral status of church members was seen as theologically irrelevant because a theological distinction between the body and soul, in which the low moral status reflected the deeds of the body but not the soul: while the body sinned, the soul remained pure. Joanna P. Moore, a northern Baptist missionary to African Americans and a contemporary of Mason, commented on this distinction:

> Some taught that this old body sinned but the soul did not sin; for example at a funeral I heard a minister say, "There lies Sister Jane; her tongue often told lies, but her soul never sinned." They got this doctrine from a false interpretation of the seventh chapter of Romans.[4]

Based on a reading of the 7th chapter of Romans, this interpretation intertwined justification with the perseverance of the saints; it became cast in the phrases "eternal security" and "once saved, always saved." To overcome this theological dilemma, Mason engaged the Black Baptist, Black Restorationist, African American Holiness, and Black Pentecostal faiths.[5]

Engaging the Theological Journey

Mason's journey through the world of the Black Baptist, Black Restorationist, African American Holiness, and Black Pentecostal faiths provided him with theological tools to learn about God's transformation of the world. In a sense, Mason's theological journey reflected his desire "to return to the old homestead," a desire that located comfort in the language of the Restorationist, Holiness, and Pentecostal faiths.

The Black Baptist faith drew upon the historic doctrines of the Christian Church, especially as expressed in the New Hampshire Baptist Confession (1833). This confession included 17 articles of the Christian faith: Scripture, the true God, the fall of man, the way of salvation, justification, freeness of salvation, grace in regeneration, God's purpose of grace, sanctification, the perseverance of saints, the harmony of law and gospel, the gospel church, baptism and the Lord's Supper, the Christian Sabbath, civil government, the righteous and the wicked, and the world to come. The faith also interwove the role of dreams and visions as a source of spiritual knowledge, premonitions, and revelations; through dreams and visions, people were converted by God into the Christian faith.

Squarely, a theology of racial equality grounded in the "Father of God and the Brotherhood of Man" and God being "no respecter of persons" informed their theological perspective.[6]

While Baptist doctrine reinforced what he saw as the moral compromise of the church, Baptist doctrine would have to withstand the scrutiny of Scripture as taught by the Black Restorationists. William Christian and his Black Restorationist movement provided the first shift within Mason's Black Baptist faith during the early 1890s. Drawing upon the larger Restorationist movement of William Campbell and Barton Stone, William Christian's motto was, "No Creed but Christ; no book but the Bible." Christian's focus encompassed the primacy of Scripture over Baptist doctrine, repentance as the focus of conversion rather than "godly sorrow" and dramatic religious experiences, the Lord's prayer as the sole Christian prayer, living a clean life as crucial as justification within the Christian faith, the concept of private property as antithetical to Scripture, and biblical names for congregations such as Church of the Living God replacing the words "Baptist" and "Methodist." Exposure to this shift led Mason to rethink his understanding of Baptist faith and reorder his theological priorities.[7]

The Black Restorationist faith pursued the quest for the recovery of the New Testament teachings, spirituality, and polity with its focus on biblical knowledge, Christian practices constituting a holy life, ecclesiology of nondenominationalism, and names borrowed from Scripture for congregations and associations of congregations. While Mason participated in the Black Restorationist movement, it never led to his withdrawal from the Baptist Church. Mason did incorporate some aspects of Black Restorationist theology into his theology.

As the Black Restorationists taught, the Bible commands clean living. With his "Bible is right" stance, Mason needed to discover a theological alternative to the Baptist doctrine of justification and perseverance of the saints. The Black Restorationists rejected the theological distinction between body and soul in regards to justification: the deeds of the body *do* have an effect on the soul; the body and soul are interrelated in regards to salvation. From the Black Restorationists, Mason latched onto the centrality of repentance for the sinner and the Christian: both must confess and repent of their sins; for the sinners, they repent unto salvation; for the Christians, they repent to be restored to God. Yet, the weight of living clean rested on the Christian.[8]

William Christian's theology of the races disavowed racial prejudice and advanced racial equality. Undergirded by a polygenesis theory that lodged the origins of the African race in the biblical creation story and identified Africans as the majority of the biblical peoples, including the Hebrews, it espoused the creation of the Asian and European races as separate events. His theology of the races refuted the interpretation of the Hamitic curse as the genesis of Black inferiority by redefining the curse as an intra-African, not interracial, affair. Thus he espoused racial equality by countering White racial superiority without substituting it with Black racial superiority.[9]

Between 1893 and 1897, Mason adopted a focus on clean or holy life and the primacy of Scripture over denominational doctrine. In 1894 and 1895, Mason's association with the Black Restorationist movement was coupled with his enrollment in the Ministers' Institute of the Arkansas Baptist College where he was taught Baptist doctrine, trained in the practice of ministry in an academic context, and graduated in 1895. The theological environment of the Ministers' Institute, sponsored by Arkansas Baptist College, aided Mason in his theological development by providing him with formal instruction in the basics of Christian doctrine, especially as articulated in the *New Hampshire Baptist Confession*, which gave him a theological framework to engage the theological ferment that he was encountering.[10]

In 1895, after ceasing his association with William Christian's movement, Mason forged within Baptist state conventions of the mid-South a Holiness trajectory, a trajectory blazed by Charles Price Jones, Walter S. Pleasant, and Mason. This Holiness trajectory promoted the teaching of Holiness, Scripture's primacy, and healing; Holiness was taught as a synonym of sanctification and the Baptism of the Holy Spirit. To Mason, the cleansing motif dominated his discourse on sanctification; the theme of cleansing overshadowed the themes of empowerment, higher life, and victorious living; he emphasized sin being cleansed in general, rather than being eradicated–as did the Wesleyans–or suppressed–as did the Keswickians.[11]

The African American Holiness faith resonated with the Restorationist quest for holy living; the Holiness faith advanced its focus through the doctrines of sanctification and healing.

From the African American Holiness faith, Mason learned that the weight of the Christian's living a clean life rested on God: "grace brings" holiness and "God wholly sanctifies." Living a clean life is a consequence of sanctification as a divine work of grace. For Jones, the major Black Holiness theologian within the circle that Mason was part of, Christ was central in the doctrine of sanctification: by being sanctified in Christ, the believer is "cleansed by His pure word; through Christ dwelling within Christians, they are kept 'sin-free.'" Christ bestowed the "power to live above sin" and offered "cleanliness and then power to keep clean." Through justification, Christ has put away the sins of the believer; through sanctification, Christ will keep the believer from "going astray." With an emphasis on the atonement or the finished work of Christ, according to the theologian Dale Irvin, Jones argued that "Christ's death removed both our sins and our sinful nature." Jones admonished Christians to "trust the atonement" made by Christ to receive "sanctification by faith."[12]

From a Holiness perspective, Mason also saw the role of discipline as a means of restoring the backslidden to fellowship with God and fellow Christians, discouraging others from backsliding, maintaining the integrity of the assembly, and protecting the reputation of the church to advance evangelism. Related to discipline was the role of exclusion or the withdrawal of "the right hand of fellowship," in which individuals were excluded from a congregation because of immorality, sloth, heresy, or unruliness.

The embrace of the Black Restorationist teaching about the biblical requirement for Scriptural names for congregations rather than the extra-biblical names of "Baptist" or "Methodist" surfaced in Mason's ministry with the chartering of the Holiness congregation established by Mason in Lexington, Mississippi, and the renaming of Baptist congregations pastored by Mason's group of associates throughout the mid-South. In addition, Mason and his associates cast this search for biblical names in terms of nondenominationalism; in the words of Charles Price Jones: "Nowhere in Holy Writ is the church called a Baptist Church."[13]

Jones carved out space within his Holiness theology to grapple with racial prejudice, racial repression, racial despair and fear, racial self-hatred, and racial victimization as theological problems. Jones advocated the justice of God, the redemption of Africa, and "political hope" as theological categories to craft a theology of racial justice. For Jones, the justice of God grew out of his interpretation of God's role in two historical events: the Exodus involving the freeing of the Hebrews, and the emancipation comprising the freeing of enslaved Africans. The redemption of Africa, with a spotlight on Egypt, Ethiopia, and Liberia, focused on the role of Christians restoring Africa as a great civilization. The nation of Israel in Scripture served as a model of the combining of religion and "political hope."[14]

Initially, Mason and his associates worked diligently within the Baptist state conventions, seeking to bring about reform; they did not want to withdraw from the Baptist movement. However, among the Baptists an opposition to the Holiness trajectory within the Baptist churches, especially its anti-denominationalism and sanctification teachings, arose that sought the disfellowshiping of Mason, Jones, and others. By 1900 this battle and disfellowshiping of Mason, Jones, and others led to Mason and his associates forming new ecclesial organizations fashioned around nondenominationalism on the district and state levels.

The Holiness movement in the mid-South heard about the Pentecostal revival in Los Angeles during 1906. In early 1907, Mason traveled to Los Angeles, along with David J. Young and John A. Jeter, to ascertain the biblical validity of the revival. The Black Pentecostal faith promoted the revised teaching about the Baptism of the Holy Spirit, distinguished from sanctification, as connected to spiritual empowerment and gifting, including the gift of speaking in tongues. From the Pentecostal faith, Mason understood that whereas grace brings sanctification, through the Baptism of the Holy Spirit, the believer receives the power to live holy, to live the life that God has ordained for and initiated in the believer. According to Jacobsen, speaking in tongues "was seen as a valid sign of the baptism of the Spirit only if recipients showed other evidence of God's loving and redemptive influence in their lives."[15]

Embracing the Theological Journey: The Formation of COGIC Doctrine

During Bishop Mason's lifetime, the Church of God in Christ published three key doctrinal statements. By 1909, a brief theological statement on God was published. This statement discussed the Trinity: the Father, the Son, and the Holy Spirit. The Church of God in Christ during the 1910s was concerned about the proliferation of doctrines among Pentecostals. The church began to take a conservative posture regarding new revelations or teaching. They began to teach: "Neither is it best for the saints of God to flirt with every new theory or strange doctrine that comes out." The Church of God in Christ defined its theological task as "to promulgate the doctrines of Christianity as taught in the [O]ld and [N]ew [T]estaments."[16]

By the late 1910s, the Church of God in Christ produced a theological statement that consisted of nine topics and was prefaced with "We Believe," and addressed the following subjects:[17]

The Gospel Alone
Salvation
Freedom from Sin
Grace and the Godly Life
Sanctification
Great Commission and Signs
Water Baptism
Baptism of the Holy Ghost
Divine Healing

By 1918, the brief theological statement from around 1909 was expanded to include such topics as fallen nature, the Baptism of the Holy Spirit, water baptism, the second coming of Christ, Sabbath, General Church Officers, Church property, and political government.

The expanded 1909 theological statement included the earlier section on the Trinity. Its statement on the fatherhood of God quoted from the Nicene Creed with the phrase "God, the Father, Almighty," and echoed the Creed by confessing God as "the Author and Creator of all things." The Christology statement professed that "Jesus Christ, was and is, the Son of God" who is "co-equal in wisdom, power and holiness, with the Father" and through Christ's "atonement the world is saved from sin and reconciled to God." The pneumatological statement confessed the co-equality within the Trinity by including the Holy Spirit being "co-equal in power with the Father and Son." Following the Western version of the Nicene Creed, the statement confessed that the Holy Spirit "proceedeth from the Father and the Son." The statement drew from other secular sources to acknowledge the Holy Spirit as the "Executive of the Trinity" with the responsibility of implementing "the plan of salvation."[18]

In the expanded version of the 1909 theological statement, the theological anthropology statement highlighted that humanity "by nature is sinful and unholy" because of the Fall and "needs to be born again, sanctified and cleansed from all sin by the Blood of Christ," stressing that Christ's blood justifies and sanctifies, recognizing Jesus as the Savior and Sanctifier. In the soteriological statement people are "saved by confessing and forsaking" their sins, here the theme of repentance as a response to the salvific work of Christ was inserted. While the focus of the statements was the work of Christ, the theology of sin shaped the section by noting the fallen nature, role of the atonement in the redemption of fallen nature, and human response of "confessing and forsaking sins." Within this theological vision, the Baptism of the Holy Spirit is "the inheritance" of the redeemed as the members of "the family of God."[19]

The theology of the Baptism of the Holy Spirit is couched within a larger theology of the Holy Spirit. The Holy Spirit is recognized as being instrumental in salvation, wherein a person is "born of the Spirit" and the Holy Spirit is active in the lives of all Christians. The distinction is made between having the Spirit through the new birth and having the "full baptism of the Holy Spirit" recorded in the Pentecost account where "speaking in tongues" is present.[20]

While this statement only includes one ordinance, water baptism, as opposed to the three discussed above in the other theological statement of the 1910s, it does recognize Sunday as the Christian Sabbath and the fact of the Second Coming; the Second Coming is framed in terms of Christ "reign[ing] on the earth in millennial power and glory" and the rapture of the church; this hope is to be held not by calculating the date of the Second Coming, but by Christians seeking "to purify themselves as He [Christ] is pure."

Holiness served as the theological motif of the statement. The "gospel alone" statement integrated words and deeds or belief with actions, acknowledging that "the only way to be Christian is to believe the gospel of Jesus and live as He commands you." The salvation statement confessed that "Jesus saves His people from sin." The saving from sin is coupled with the believer being free from sin; the third statement highlighted that those who are "born of God" do not "commit sin." The ability to live free from sin is by God's grace; God's grace wholly sanctifies the Christian, wholly encompasses "body, soul, and spirit." The body, soul, and spirit are transformed through sanctification. The Great Commission was yoked to the Great Signs, which link holiness, evangelism, baptizing, preaching, and charismatic signs. The theology concluded with three statements that were pulled out of the Great Commission and Signs: water baptism by immersion as the biblical form, the Baptism with the Holy Ghost as the "gift of power," and "divine healing in answer to the prayer of faith and laying on of hands."[21]

In 1928, the General Assembly included the expanded doctrinal statement within the Constitution. The General Assembly in 1926/27 approved of seven doctrines. These doctrines were Trinity–including The Father, The Son, and The Holy Spirit; Fallen Nature; Baptism of the Holy Spirit; Water Baptism, The Second Coming of Christ; The Sabbath; and Political Government. Each topic began and included the phrase: "We believe."[22]

Earlier during the 1924 General Assembly the delegates agreed to teach an array of Christian doctrine from a Church of God in Christ perspective. These topics were:[23]

- Fatherhood of God
- Sonship of Christ
- Repentance
- Faith
- Conversion
- Regeneration
- Justification
- Sanctification
- Baptism of the Holy Ghost
- Divine Healing
- Laying on of hands
- Restoration millennium reign, the white throne of judgment
- Marriage
- Ordinance of the Church: water Baptism, foot washing, Lord's Supper, tithing & etc.
- Church Governments

During the 1924 General Assembly, COGIC adopted Bishop Mason's model of theological dialogue. They voted to commit three or four days to theological education. At these sessions, the ministers and missionaries would come together to be taught from their Bibles "the Doctrine of the Church in subjects" such as the Trinity, justification, sanctification, the Baptism of the Holy Ghost, and the

Second Coming of Christ. They adopted this model because by the 1920s COGIC ministers had come from "almost every denomination" and had "been taught all kinds of Doctrines contrary to that of the Church of God in Christ" in these other denominations. Consequently, they instituted a theological forum for COGIC ministers to debate and discuss the biblical basis of the doctrine.[24]

In the 1930s, the first edition of the COGIC manual was published with a set of Articles of Religion. The Articles of Religion presented COGIC teachings about 15 doctrinal subjects; most of these topics had been selected at the 1924 General Assembly. During the 1930s, COGIC published its first set of "Articles of Religion," in which the doctrines of the Trinity, Scripture, Creation, the Church, Justification, Sanctification, the Baptism of the Holy Ghost, the Second Coming, and other topics were discussed. These documents and the theological development that these documents reflect constituted the core of Mason's theological legacy.[25]

Scripture

Early in his ministry, Mason referred to the "Bible as my sacred guide." The Bible was a holy book that would orient the Christian life. Mason experienced the transformative power of the "word of God" to sanctify people. Mason defined Scripture as, "Scriptures are signs of the only Christ, the glory of God. From the Scriptures Jesus spoke to the minds of the people, and they looked to Him and marveled." Scripture as signs resonates with his understanding of Scripture as a "sacred guide." The primary purpose of Scripture was revelation of Jesus Christ. Mason also recognized that the Hebrew Scriptures that Jesus used in preaching become extended to the New Testament writings to constitute the Bible. In 1927, the Church of God in Christ confessed a theology of Scripture that upheld the integrity of Holy Scripture as one book of two testaments and defined Scripture "as our rule of faith and practice," focusing on the role of Scripture in ordering the Christian life and community.[26]

Bishop Mason was unafraid of theological controversy. He permitted different doctrinal positions to be debated in special theological forums. He even recognized that theological differences did exist within COGIC. He taught that the existence of theological differences had existed since biblical times; these differences could cause confusion and division. According to him, the New Testament church at times needed to be put back in order by the apostles, men called by God to lead the church.[27]

COGIC doctrinal statements were situated within a theological framework that addressed racial prejudice, lynching, and war as theological problems. While war as a theological problem was included in the statements, racial prejudice and lynching were challenged in other documents such as sermons and books. According to James Courts, Mason demonstrated through Scripture that the resolution to the race problems of Mason's era required "patience, prayers and supplication to God" more than "patience and co-operation of the North and South"; racial prejudice was more of a spiritual than social problem, demanding a spiritual solution. Lynching occurred because Christians were cowards in the face of this injustice, a cowardice resulting from lacking the Baptism of the Holy Spirit, who bestowed courage and power. Mason's theology of racial equality was grounded in "all believers are one in Christ Jesus and all its members have equal rights." This theology of racial equality lodged its basis in the intersection of Christology and ecclesiology rather than the Black Baptist emphasis on the intersection of doctrines of God and anthropology (or humanity), or the Black Restorationist polygenesis theory.[28]

Enabling the Theological Journey: Crafting an Approach to Doctrine

In both the writings of Bishop Mason and the early theological documents of the Church of God in Christ, there is evidence of a clear biblical approach to doctrine. Five elements constitute the biblical approach. This approach can be described in the following way. First, the Bible must be the key source for all doctrine. The Scriptures are "rule of faith and practice." Doctrine can only be based on clear statements within Scripture. All doctrines should have support from both the Old and New Testaments. With support from both Testaments, doctrine will not be based on one Bible verse. Bishop Mason always listed and discussed scriptures from both Testaments to base doctrine. By studying scriptures in both Testaments, he protected the Church from developing doctrine that contradicted the whole of Scripture.[29]

Second, doctrine communicates the biblical understanding of God and God's work in the world. Doctrine is the place to discuss only particular topics; every subject is not a topic for doctrine. For instance, COGIC was clear about its Christian code of conduct and dress, and many sermons were preached on conduct and dress. Yet the COGIC Christian code of conduct and dress were never included within its doctrinal statements. COGIC differentiated between doctrine and general teaching. COGIC followed the precedent set in Hebrews 6, in which the essential doctrines are identified. It was important to distinguish what was "necessary to salvation" and what was not essential for salvation. According to the COGIC teaching:

> The Holy Scriptures contain all things necessary to salvation and is a complete and infallible guide and standard of authority in all matters of religion and morals; therefore whatever it teaches is to be believed and whatever it commands is to obeyed, and whatever it condemns is to be renounced as both wrong and sinful; and whatever is not read therein, nor may be proven thereby, is not to be required of any man as necessary to salvation. 2nd Tim. 3:16–17.[30]

Third, COGIC was clear that "whatever is not read" and fails to be proven in Scripture "is not to be required of any man as necessary to salvation." With the Bible as primary, the church is able to resist the temptation to develop doctrine out of vain speculations. What is also clear is that where the Bible is silent, doctrine must also be silent.

Fourth, biblical themes formed the core of the doctrinal topics such as Creation, Revelation, Inspiration of Scripture, God, Salvation, Sanctification, and Church. On one hand, Bishop Mason made sure that only a particular set of topics were classified as doctrine and protected the Church, making every topic a doctrine. On the other hand, many of the select biblical themes that serve as COGIC doctrinal topics had also been topics that Christians, since the New Testament Church, had also selected. This allows for a theological dialogue between COGIC doctrine and the doctrine of other churches throughout the history of Christianity.[31]

Fifth, doctrine is to be lived and practiced as well as believed. Doctrine must be more than an intellectual exercise or an abstract activity; biblical doctrine shapes the Christian life. Whatever doctrine Scripture "teaches is to be believed and whatever it commands is to be obeyed." For Bishop Mason, biblically based doctrine could transform lives by the power of the Holy Spirit.

These five elements to the COGIC biblical approach to doctrine set the Church on a course that avoided experimenting with the latest doctrines that were preached just because they were new. COGIC remained committed to wrestling with the Scriptures to discover the doctrine of Christ.

Mason's Doctrinal Teaching in the Context of Protestantism

During Bishop Mason's lifetime, various theological options captured the imagination of many churches. While churches debated theological perspectives that ranged from dispensationalism to fundamentalism to liberalism, Bishop Mason remained committed to focusing on the Bible. Bishop Mason's aim was to obey and preach the Bible. Navigating the context shaped by evidentiary tongues, fundamentalism, oneness doctrine of the Godhead, Christians never die, nonobservance of Christian holidays/holy days (Christmas and Easter), Mason sought to be biblically based, rather than be the disciple of every new religious movement or theological curiosity.

Mason explored the debate surrounding the number of ordinances of the Church. Are there two or three? According to those who contended for two ordinances, such as many Baptists and Methodists, water baptism and the Lord's Supper were the only two, while for those who contended for three ordinances, foot washing was added to the list. Mason challenged his Methodist counterparts as his Baptist associates would on whether baptism had to by total immersion; he challenged Black Restorationists by agreeing with the Baptists and Methodists that the drink in the Lord's Supper was wine (or grape juice) and not water; and he challenged his Baptist and Methodist counterparts by contending that their list of ordinances was incomplete by omitting foot washing.

Dispensationalism was popular in Bishop Mason's era, popularized by the *Scofield Reference Bible*, which was first published in 1909. Dispensationalists divided biblical history into these seven dispensations or ages: the Age of Innocence, the Age of Conscience, the Age of Human Government, the Age of Promise, the Age of Law, the Age of Grace, and the Age of the Millennium. In ordering biblical history into dispensations, dispensationalists claimed that certain activities were restricted to specific dispensations. Miracles, according to dispensationalists, ended with the death of the first apostles. Yet Bishop Mason taught that miracles still happened today. He testified about how God used him in the healing ministry. For dispensationalists, what God did in the first five dispensations became interpreted as biblical information about the past. Bishop Mason read the Bible as a whole and he looked for references in the Old and New Testaments to understand the biblical teaching on Holiness, for instance. Bishop Mason did not divide God's activity in periods. Rather than divide the Bible into dispensations, Bishop Mason focused on the message that the Bible was proclaiming.[32]

The fundamentalists were another Christian group that gained popularity during Bishop Mason's time. As a matter of fact, some fundamentalist were even dispensationalists. The fundamentalists emphasized five fundamentals: (1) the verbal inerrancy of Scripture, (2) the divinity of Jesus, (3) the virgin birth of Jesus, (4) salvation as substitutionary atonement, and (5) the physical resurrection and the bodily return of Jesus; these five fundamentals were popularized by the multi-volume book series called *The Fundamentals.* Of concern to Christians such as Bishop Mason was why the fundamentalists did not include sanctification, since this doctrine was in the Bible. Bishop Mason also disagreed with the fundamentalist teaching that "speaking in tongues" was demonic; Bishop Mason saw that the Bible defended "speaking in tongues." Rather than follow the fundamentalists with their discussions of the inerrancy of Scripture, Bishop Mason adopted biblical language to communicate a biblical view of the authority of Scripture.[33]

Fundamentalists and dispensationalists also placed a lot of emphasis on interpreting the Last Days. The books of Daniel, Ezekiel, and Revelations were central to their debates about Armageddon, pre-tribulation and post-tribulation, and other topics. Bishop Mason placed his emphasis on Jesus' return, warning people to be ready. He resisted speculating about the details of the Last Days. Rather than emphasize the Beast and the mark of the Beast, for example, Bishop Mason focused on Jesus and what the Bible said about Jesus' coming again. He admonished "all who have this hope in them to purify themselves as He is pure (1 Jn. 3:3)." Bishop Mason's perspective on the Second Coming was Christ-centered.

Among Pentecostals there were three major debates. The first debate centered around the relationship between the Baptism of the Holy Spirit and the act of speaking in tongues. While some Pentecostals described the relationship in terms of initial evidence, Bishop Mason resisted the temptation to introduce foreign terms such as initial evidence and evidentiary tongues to discuss the Baptism of the Holy Spirit. He led COGIC to employ the biblical terms "sign" and "seal." He borrowed the language of "sign" from Mark 16:17 and "seal" from Ephesians 1:13. For Mason, love was central to living the life empowered by the Holy Spirit.[34]

A second debate among Pentecostals explored whether people needed the Baptism of the Holy Spirit to be saved, and did people only receive the Holy Spirit when they were Baptized with the Holy Spirit. Salvation occurs from being born of the Spirit, Mason taught. One is first saved prior to the Baptism of the Holy Spirit. We are not baptized with the Spirit to be saved, but we are baptized with the Spirit because we are [already] saved, Mason said. Thus, a distinction was made between salvation as "being born of the Spirit" according to John 3:5 and the baptism as "being baptized with the Spirit" according to Acts 2:4. COGIC leaders made clear that they did "not presume to teach that no one has the Spirit that does not speak in tongues" or "that we are baptized with the Spirit in order to be saved." COGIC contended that "a full baptism of the Holy Ghost as poured out on the day of Pentecost is accompanied by the speaking in tongues."[35]

A third debate among Pentecostals involved interpretations about the doctrine of God. In the early theology statement, COGIC used the term "Trinity" to refer to the "three-in-oneness." Bishop Mason referred to 1 John 5:7 to note that there were "three in the Godhead" and these three are one. He proclaimed the unity of God. He noted that the verse said, "For there are three that bear record in heaven" (KJV). These three are Father, Word, and Holy Ghost, and, according to Scripture, "these three are one." By focusing on John 1:1–18, Bishop Mason taught that the Father, Son, and Holy Spirit were not three Gods, but one God, And that Jesus was, according to John 1:14 and 3:16, the "only begotten son" of the Father.[36]

Mason's theological journey crafted a theological vision that enabled him to reconstruct a Christian community in which "a religion like that he heard the old folks talk about and manifest in their lives" would be practiced. His theology was informed by language and concepts from the Black Restorationist, Black American

Holiness, and Black Pentecostal faiths. Instead of the church being a mixed assembly in which spiritual and carnal Christians as well as unrepentant sinners or backslidden Christians predominate, Mason sought to build a church in which the believers exhibit the sanctifying power of God to change lives and the Pentecostal power of God to sustain transformed lives. Rather than a theology of the church shaped by the biblical metaphor of the wheat and tares growing together as means to protect the weak and safeguard against inadvertently harming the good to destroy the immoral, Mason espoused a theology of the church as an assembly of holiness Christians, an assembly that strove to be "blameless" before the world. The church must be a place of instruction, formation, and discipline.[37]

As stated above, in an early biographical account Mason noted the difference between his birthplace and homestead of his early years –which was marked by Christian qualities–and the place where his family relocated during his adolescence–an ungodly environment. His homestead was informed by "a religion like that he heard the old folks talk about and manifest in their lives." In his homestead, the congregation and community maintained a correspondence between the teaching and practice of the Christian faith; there was a correspondence between their testimony and lifestyle; the Christian faith was transformative, translating words into actions. In a sense, Mason's theological journey reflected his desire "to return to the old homestead," a desire that located comfort in the language of the Restorationist, Holiness, and Pentecostal faiths.[38]

CONCLUSION

Bishop Charles Harrison Mason bequeathed to the Church of God in Christ a profound theological foundation. His theological legacy has served the Church of God in Christ well by providing a biblical way to accomplish the command of Jude 3: "contend for the faith which was once delivered unto the saints" (KJV). In the midst of the theological controversy of the early twentieth century, he led a theological movement within the Church of God in Christ that advanced the biblical mission of the Church.

Bishop Mason taught that doctrine must be biblically based and oriented. The theological movement he led embraced biblical concepts to express the theological vision that he and the other pioneers believed communicated the message of the Bible. They promoted a biblical theology. Under his leadership, the Church of God in Christ produced a set of published doctrinal statements that grew out of his commitment to Scripture.

Bishop Mason led a theological movement in the Church of God in Christ that made the Bible pivotal to the doctrines that the Church taught. Bishop Mason taught his people to be committed to sound doctrine and COGIC avoided merely adopting the latest theologies that came along. With the five elements of his biblical approach to doctrine, Bishop Mason ensured that the Bible was central to COGIC doctrine and left a foundation on which COGIC could build. He has left a theological legacy to the Church of God in Christ that has profoundly shaped the Church immensely.

Selected Bibliography and References

Alexander, Estrelda. *Black Fire: One Hundred Years of African American Pentecostalism.* Downers Grove, Ill.: InterVarsity Press, 2011.

——. *The Women of Azusa Street.* Cleveland: Pilgrim's Press, 2005.

Anderson, Allan. "The Azusa Street Revival and the Emergence of Pentecostal Missions in the Early Twentieth Century." *Transformation 23,* no. 2 (April 2006): 107–18.

Anderson, Robert M. *Vision of the Disinherited.* Peabody, Mass.: Hendrickson Publishers, 1992.

Bartleman, Frank. *Azusa Street: The Roots of Modern Day Pentecost.* Los Angeles: Self Published. Rpt., Vinson Synan, ed., South Plainfield, N.J.: Bridge Publishing Inc., 1980.

Brewer, John Mason. *American Negro Folklore.* Chicago: Quadrangle Books, 1968.

Britton, Larry G., ed. *A Memphis Corporate Salute: Bishop Charles Harrison Mason, Founder of Church of God in Christ.* Memphis: Church of God in Christ Public Relations Department, 1994.

Burgess, Stanley M., and Gary B. McGee, eds. *Dictionary of Pentecostal and Charismatic Movements.* Grand Rapids, Mich.: Regency Reference Library, 1988.

Butler, Anthea. *Women in the Church Of God In Christ: Making a Sanctified World.* Chapel Hill, N.C.: University of North Carolina Press, 2007.

Byas, Lelia Mason. "The Life and Times of Bishop C.H. Mason" [audio recording], produced by the Historical Cultural Museum and Fine Arts Center, Church of God in Christ. Memphis: Church of God in Christ Publishing House, 1987.

Calhoun, Lillian S. "Woman on the Go for God." *Ebony Magazine* (May 1963): 78–88.

Caravantes, Peggy. *Marcus Garvey Black Nationalist.* Greensboro, N.C.: Morgan Reynolds Publisher, 2004.

Cartwright, Joseph H. *The Triumph of Jim Crow: Tennessee Race Relations in the 1880s.* Knoxville, Tenn.: The University of Tennessee Press, 1976.

Chireau, Yvonne. *Black Magic: Religion and the African American Conjuring Tradition.* Berkeley, Calif.: University of California Press, 2003.

"Church of God in Christ Celebrates 50th Anniversary: Church of God in Christ Lauds Founder." *Ebony Magazine* (March 1958): 54–60.

Church of God in Christ. *The Story of Bishop C.H. Mason and the Development of the Church of God in Christ.* Video. Memphis: Church of God in Christ Publishing Board, 1993.

Clemmons, Ithiel C. "True Koinonia: Pentecostal Hopes and Historical Realities." *Pneuma: The Journal for the Society for Pentecostal Studies* 4, no.1 (Spring 1982): 46–56.

—–. *Bishop C.H. Mason and the Roots of the Church of God in Christ.* Bakersfield, Calif.: Pneuma Life Publishing, 1996.

—–. "Shaping the Coming Era of the Church of God in Christ in Eastern New York First Jurisdiction" (MA thesis, New York Theological Seminary, 1992).

Cobbins, Otho B., ed. *History of Church of Christ (Holiness) U. S. A. 1895–1965.* New York: Vantage Press, 1966.

Coffey, Lillian Brooks, comp. [1926], *1926 Year Book of the Church of God in Christ.* Material from 1934 Year Book and other Church of God in Christ Publications added by Jerry R. Ramsey. Memphis: Church of God in Christ, 1991.

Cornelius, Lucille J., ed. *The Pioneer: History of the Church of God in Christ.* Memphis: Church of God in Christ Publishing House, 1975.

Daniels, David D. III. "The Cultural Renewal of Slave Religion: Charles Price Jones and the Emergence of the Holiness Movement in Mississippi" (Ph.D. dissertation, Union Theological Seminary, 1992).

Delk, James L. *He Made Millions of People Happy.* Hopkinsville, Ky.: privately printed, 1945.

Dempster, Murray W., Byron D. Klaus, and Douglas Petersen, eds. *The Globalization of Pentecostalism: A Religion Made to Travel.* Irvine, Calif.: Regnum Books, 1999.

Du Bois, W.E.B. *The Souls of Black Folks.* New York: Fawcett Publications, 1961. First published 1903 by A.C. McClurg & Co.

Evans, James Jr. *We Have Been Believers: An African American Systematic Theology.* Minneapolis: Fortress Press, 1992.

Faulkner, Juanita W., and Raynard D. Smith, eds., *Book of Minutes: 1919–1933* (in press).

Frank, Andrew F. *The Routledge Historical Atlas of the American South.* New York: Routledge, 1999.

Franklin, John Hope, and Alfred A. Moss Jr. *From Slavery to Freedom: A History of African Americans.* 7th ed. New York: McGraw-Hill Inc., 1994.

Franklin, Robert M. *Another Day's Journey: Black Churches Confronting the American Crisis.* Minneapolis: Fortress Press, 1997.

Frazier, E. Franklin. *The Negro Church in America.* New York: Schocken Books, 1974.

Fulop, Timothy E., and Albert J. Raboteau, eds. *African-American Religion: Interpretive Essays in History and Culture.* New York: Routledge, 1997.

Giggie, John M. *After Redemption: Jim Crow and the Transformation of African American Religion in the Delta, 1875–1915.* New York: Oxford University Press, 2008.

Gilkes, Cheryl Townsend. *If It Wasn't for the Women.* New York: Orbis Press, 2000.

Goff, James, and Grant Wacker, eds. *Portraits of a Generation: Early Pentecostal Leaders.* Fayetteville, Ark.: University of Arkansas Press, 2002.

Goodson, Glenda Williams. *Bishop Mason and Those Sanctified Women!* Dallas, Tex.: HCM Publishing, 2003.

——. *The Making of a Legend.* Dallas, Tex.: HCM Publishing, 2006.

Hall, Alferd Z. *So You Want to Know Your Church?* Memphis: Zannju Publishing, 1995.

Harris, J. William. "Etiquette, Lynching, and Racial Boundaries in Southern History: A Mississippi Example." *American Historical Review*, Vol. 100, No. 2 (Apr.1995): 387–410.

Higginbotham, Evelyn Brooks. *Righteous Discontent: Women's Movement in the Black Church, 1880–1920.* Cambridge, Mass.: Harvard University Press, 1986.

Hurston, Zora Neale. *The Sanctified Church.* New York: Marlowe & Company, 1981.

Johnson, Clifton H. *God Struck Me Dead: Voices of Ex-slaves.* Cleveland: Pilgrim Press, 1993.

Jones, Charles Edwin, *Black Holiness: A Guide to the Study of Black Participation in Wesleyan Perfectionist and Glossolalic Pentecostal Movements.* Metuchen, N.J.: Scarecrow Press, Inc., 1987.

Jones, Charles Price. "A Message of Hope for the Black Man: How He May Get Thro [sic] This Awful Time." *Truth.* (December, 1903).

Kornweibel Jr., Theodore. "Bishop C.H. Mason and the Church of God in Christ During World War I: The Perils of Conscientious Objection." *Southern Studies: An Interdisciplinary Journal of the South*, 26, (Fall 1987): 273–78.

Lamon, Lester C. *Blacks in Tennessee 1791–1970.* Knoxville, Tenn.: University of Tennessee Press, 1977.

Lee, Elnora L. C.H. *Mason: A Man Greatly Used of God.* Women's Department, Church of God in Christ:. Memphis, 1967.

Levine, Lawrence W. *Black Culture and Black Consciousness: Afro-American Folk Thought from Slavery to Freedom.* New York: Oxford University Press, 1978.

Lincoln, C. Eric, and Lawrence H. Mamiya. *The Black Church in the African American Experience.* Durham, N.C.: Duke University Press, 1990.

Lipford, Jesse E. "Sanctifying the Unholy: Black Pentecostalism, the Church of God in Christ and African American Culture." *West Tennessee Journal of History Society* 56 (Spring 2000): 40.

Litwack, Leon F. *Been in the Storm So Long: The Aftermath of Slavery.* New York: Vintage Books, 1980.

Lovett, Leonard, "Black Holiness-Pentecostalism: Implications for Ethics and Social Transformation." (Ph.D. Diss., Emory, 1978).

Lutz, Norma Jean. *History of the Black Church.* Philadelphia: Chelsea House Publishers, 2001.

MacRobert, Iain. *The Black Roots and White Racism of Early Pentecostalism in the USA.* Eugene, Oreg.: Wipf and Stock Publishers, 2003.

Mason, Elsie W., ed. *The Man, Charles Harrison Mason: 1866–1961.* Memphis: Church of God in Christ Publishing House, 1979.

Mason, Mary. *The History and Life Work of Elder C.H. Mason and His Co-laborers.* rpt, 1924. Memphis: Church of God in Christ Publishing Board, 1987.

Maxwell, Joe. "Building the Church." *Christianity Today,* April 8, 1996, 22–23, 25–28.

Mbiti, John S. *African Religions and Philosophy.* Garden City, N.Y.: Doubleday, 1970.

McBride, Calvin S. *Walking in a New Spirituality: Chronicling the Life, Ministry, and Contributions of Elder Robert E. Hart, B.D., LL.B., D.D. to the CME Church and COGIC.* Lincoln, Neb.: iUniverse Inc., 2007.

——. *Frank Avant vs. C.H. Mason: Mason and the Holy Ghost on Trial.* New York: iUniverse, Inc., 2009.

Mitchell, Henry H. *Black Preaching.* New York: J.B. Lippincott Company, 1970.

Moore, Allie T. *Bishop C. H. Mason Singing, Preaching and Praying in the Spirit,* vol.1, CD. LaVergne, Tenn.: Altmo Productions, 2012.

Morring, R. *Mason Memorial Church of God in Christ: 90th Church Anniversary.* Norfolk, Va.: Mason Memorial COGIC, 1996.

Murphy, Larry G., ed., *Down by the Riverside: Readings in African American Religion.* New York: New York University Press, 2000.

Nelson, Douglas J. "For Such a Time as This: The Study of Bishop William J. Seymour and the Azusa Street Revival" (Ph.D. dissertation, University of Birmingham, 1981).

Niebuhr, H. Richard. *Christ and Culture.* London, England: Faber & Faber Limited, 1952.

Noble, Myron, ed. *Like as of Fire.* Washington, D.C.: Middle Atlantic Regional Press, 1985.

"Opinion." *The Whole Truth* (April, 1968): 6.

Owens, Robert R. *Speak to the Rock.* Lanham, Md.: The University Press of America, 1998.

——. *Never Forget!: The Dark Years of COGIC History.* Longwood, Fla.. Xulon Publishing, 2001.

Paris, Peter. *Black Religious Leaders: Conflict in Unity.* Louisville, Ky.: Westminster/John Knox Press, 1991.

——. *The Social Teachings of the Black Churches.* Philadelphia: Fortress Press, 1985.

——. "The Bible and the Black Churches." *The Bible and Social Reform*, ed., E. Sandeen. Philadelphia: Fortress Press, 1982.

Park, Eunjin. *"White" Americans in "Black" Africa: Black and White American Methodist Missionaries in Liberia, 1820–1875*, Graham Russell Hodges, gen. ed. New York:, Routledge Press, 2001.

Patterson, James O., Ross, German K., and Atkins, Julia M. (eds.). *History and the Formative Years of the Church of God in Christ.* Memphis: Church of God in Christ Publishing House, 1969.

Pleas, Charles H. *Fifty Years Achievement From 1906–1956: A Period in History of the Church of God in Christ.* Memphis: Church of God in Christ Public Relations, 1991.

Porter, Andrew, *Religion Versus Empire? British Protestant Missionaries and Overseas Expansion, 1700–1914.* Manchester, UK: University of Manchester Press: 2004.

Puckett, Newbell Niles. [1926]. *Folk Beliefs of the Southern Negro.* Chapel Hill, N.C.: University of North Carolina Press, 1968.

Quarles, Benjamin. *The Negro in the Making of America.* New York: Macmillan Publishing Co., 1969.

Raboteau, Albert J. *Slave Religion: The Invisible Institution in the Antebellum South.* New York: Oxford University Press, 1978.

Ramsey, Jerry. *The Late Apostle C.H. Mason Speaks.* Privately printed, n.d.

Reagan, Charles Wilson, and William Ferris, eds. *Encyclopedia of Southern Culture.* Chapel Hill, N.C.: University of North Carolina Press, 1998.

Robeck, Cecil M., Jr. *Azusa Street Mission and Revival: The Birth of the Global Pentecostal Movement.* Nashville: Thomas Nelson Inc., 2006.

Saheed A. Adejumobi. "The Pan-African Congress," in *Organizing Black America: An Encyclopedia of Black Associations*, Nina Mjagkij, ed. New York: Garland Publishing, Inc., 2001.

Sanders, Cheryl J. "History of Women in the Pentecostal Movement," *Cyberjournal for Pentecostal-Charismatic Research*, 1996. Available at http://www.pctii.org/cyberj/cyberj2/SANDERS.pdf.

——. *Saints in Exile: The Holiness-Pentecostal Experience in African American Religion and Culture.* New York: Oxford University Press, 1996.

Simmons, Dovie Marie, and Olivia L. Martin. *Down Behind the Sun: The Story of Arenia Conella Mallory.* Memphis: Riverside Press, 1983.

Sobel, Mechal. *Trabelin' On: The Slave Journey to an Afro-Baptist Faith.* Westport, Conn.: Greenwood Press, 1979.

Spann, Billie Roberts. *The Role of Women in the Church from the Creation to Modern Day Denominational Practice*, Baltimore: Umoja Community Development Corporation, 2010.

Synan, Vinson. *The Century of the Holy Spirit.* Nashville: Thomas Nelson, 2001.

——. *The Holiness-Pentecostal Tradition: Charismatic Movements in the Twentieth Century.* Grand Rapids, Mich.: William B. Eerdmans Publishers, 1997.

——, ed. *Aspects of Pentecostal-Charismatic Origins.* Plainfield, N.J.: Logos, 1997.

——. "The Quiet Rise of Black Pentecostals." *Charisma* (June 1986): 45–48.

The Schomburg Center for Research in Black Culture, "The Colonization of Liberia, *In Motion, : The African-American Migration Experience.* www.inmotionaame.org.

Tillich, Paul. "Religious Symbols and Our Knowledge of God." *The Christian Scholar* 38, no. 3 (September 1955): 189–97.

Townes, Emilie M. *Womanist Justice, Womanist Hope.* Atlanta: Scholars Press, 1993.

Troutman, Joseph E., ed. *The Journal of the Interdenominational Theological Center.* Atlanta: ITC Press, 1987.

Tucker, David M. *Black Pastors and Leaders: Memphis, 1819–1972.* Memphis: Memphis State University Press, 1975.

U.S. Department of Commerce. *We the Americans: Blacks.* Washington, D.C.: Government Printing Office, September, 1993.

——. *Population Change and Distribution: 1990 to 2000* [C2KBR/01-2]. Table 2: "Population Change and 2000 Share by Metropolitan Status and Size Category: 1990 to 2000." Washington, D.C.: Government Printing Office, April, 2001.

——. *The Black Population in the United States: March 2002.* Figure 2: "Metropolitan and Nonmetropolitan Residence by Race: 2002." Washington, D.C.: Government Printing Office, April, 2003.

Wacker, Grant. *Heaven Below: Early Pentecostals and American Culture.* Cambridge, Mass.: Harvard University Press, 2001.

Weaver, Elton H., III. "The Metamorphosis of C. H. Mason: Origins of Black Pentecostals in Tennessee." Tennessee Historical Quarterly vol. 63, no. 2 (Summer 2004): 87–102.

Wells, Theda B. *Time to Remember: 100 Year Anniversary Celebration 1907–2007.* Memphis: Church Of God In Christ Publishing House, 2007.

Wharton, Vernon L. *The Negro in Mississippi 1865–1890.* New York: Harper and Row, Publishers, 1965.

White, Calvin Jr. *The Rise to Respectability: Race, Religion, and the Church of God in Christ.* Fayetteville, Ark.: The University of Arkansas Press, 2012.

Williams, J. *The Church That Jesus Builds: A Historical Perspective.* published for 85th Church Anniversary Mason Memorial Church of God in Christ, 1991.

Williams, J. Rodman. *Renewal Theology: Systematic Theology from a Charismatic Perspective.* Vol. 3: The Church, the Kingdom, and Last Things. Grand Rapids, Mich.: Zondervan, 1996.

Williams-Goodson, Glenda. "Biographical Profiles of Early Church of God in Christ Leaders," accompanying Louis F. Morgan's article "The Flame Still Burns." *Charisma* vol. 33, no. 4 (November 2007).

Young, C. Special Editorial. *85th Church Anniversary of Mason Memorial Church of God in Christ.* n.p., 1991.

Notes

Chapter 1: True Koinonia

1. This article is reprinted by permission from the Society of Pentecostal Studies and Mrs. Clara Clemmons, from *Pneuma*, vol. 4 (Spring 1982): 46–56.

2. My mentor and teacher, Dr. Henry Pitney Van Dusen, following the distinguished and prophetic Frederick Dennison Maurice, said to John L. Sherrill of *Guideposts Magazine*, "I have come to feel that the Pentecostal Movement, within its emphasis on the Holy Spirit, is more than just another revival. It is a revolution in our day. It is a revolution comparable in importance with the establishment of the original Apostolic Church and with the Protestant Reformation." Cf. John L. Sherrill, *They Speak with Other Tongues* (Old Tappan, N.J.: Fleming H. Revell Co., 1964), 30; cf. Henry Van Dusen, *Spirit, Son and Father* (New York: Scribner and Sons, 1958).

3. My church follows its founder, the late Bishop Charles Harrison Mason, in working with groups like SPS (e.g., Pentecostal World Conference, Pentecostal Fellowship of North America, etc.). Our approach is one of love and cautious optimism. It is not always clear to us what such groups mean by brotherhood or unity, yet we are open to find out.

4. Mrs. Leona Hale, a powerful leader of the Church of God in Christ in Southern California from 1913 to the time of a 1979 interview was 101 years of age at the time of that interview, in which she gave solid examples of how this movement was socially as well as religiously revolutionary. There were, for example, two men both with the same last name–Lee. Ed Lee was Black–the first man to receive the Pentecostal experience April 9, 1906, at Bonnie Brae Street. The other, Owen Lee, an Irish Catholic, was one of the first White brethren to receive the Pentecostal experience. Both of these brethren were dedicated to Brother William Seymour's vision of a Spirit-filled fellowship without barriers of face, sex, or class. Mother Hale claims that own "Irish" Lee would often groan in his spirit, longing for the glorious day he experienced at the beginning.

From a taped interview with Mother L. O. Hale (Memphis: Nov. 1979). Cf. C. W. Shumway, *A Study of the Gift of Tongues* (unpublished A.B. dissertation, University of Southern California, 1914), 17, 28.

5. Frank Bartleman, *Azusa Street* (Plainfield, N.J.: Logos International, 1980), 69. Originally published in 1925 as How Pentecost Came to Los Angeles.

6. B. F. Lawrence, *The Apostolic Faith Restored* (St. Louis Gospel Publishing House, 1916). One of the earliest chronicles from within a classical Pentecostal body.

7. Robert Mapes Anderson, *Vision of the Disinherited: The Making of American Pentecostalism* (New York: Oxford University Press, 1979) .

8. Peter Gay, *A Loss of Mastery: Puritan Historians in Colonial America* (Berkeley, Calif.: 1966), 10; quoted also in Robert T. Handy, *A Christian America: Protestant Hopes and Historical Realities* (New York: Oxford University Press, 1971), 7.

9. Walter Hollenweger, letter to Ithiel Clemmons, July 5, 1981.

10. Douglas J. Nelson, "For Such a Times as This: The Study of Bishop William J. Seymour and the Azusa Street Revival" (unpublished Ph.D. dissertation at the University of Birmingham May, 1981. Birmingham, England), 9–16, 294–96.

11. Ibid, 16.

12. Carl Brumback, *A Sound from Heaven* (Springfield, Mo.: Gospel Publishing House, 1961), cf. Nils Blch-Hoel, *The Pentecostal Movement: Origin, Development and Distinctive Character* (Oslo, Norway: Universitetfarlaget, 1964).

13. Personal conversation with Professor James Cone at Union Theological Seminary, October 21, 1981.

14. G. B. Cashwell is a classic example of such an experience and personal-social revolution.

15. Even scholars like Lovett and Tinney will have to correct the one-eyed caricature that is traced back to a racist *L.A. Times'* article of April 17, 1906. Bartleman avoids that. He truthfully states that Seymour is blind in one eye. Seymour's later photographs show that he was not one-eyed, nor did he have a glass eye. Nelson deals effectively with all caricatures of Seymour.

16. Nelson, "For Such a Time as This," op. cit., 166.

17. James L. Delk, *He Made Millions of People Happy* (Hopkinsville, Ky.: n.p., 1944), 708.

18. Ibid., 9.

CHAPTER 2: WHEN IN THE COURSE OF HUMAN EVENTS?

1. "Table Bb129-166: Slave Population by State and Sex, 1820-1860," in *Historical Statistics of the United States: Earliest Times to the Present* (New York: Cambridge University Press, 2006), 2:378. Specifically, there were 1,982,625 males reported as slaves in 1860, and 1,971,135 females.

2. "Our Foundation," *Church of God in Christ* (http://www.cogic.org/our-foundation : accessed December 31, 2012). Please note, *Yearbook of American & Canadian Churches, 2012* (Nashville: Abingdon Press, 2012), 370, reports church membership based on 1991 returns. For that year, they reported membership at 5.5 million.

3. "Finding Birth & Death Records in Tennessee," *Tennessee State Library and Archives* (http://www.tennessee.gov/tsla/history/vital/vital.htm : accessed December 31, 2012).

4. "Birth Records," *Arkansas Department of Health* (http://www.healthy.arkansas.gov/programsServices/certificatesVitalRecords/Pages/BirthRecords.aspx : accessed December 31, 2012).

5. "Finding Birth and Death Records in Tennessee," *Tennessee State Library and Archives.*

6. "Birth Records," *Arkansas Department of Health.*

7. Michigan Department of Health, certificate of death local file 14980 (1961), Charles H. Mason; City of Detroit.

8. Date of birth and death from Tennessee Department of Health, certificate of death 2006 009010 (2006), Elsie W. Washington; County Clerk, Memphis.

9. Michigan certificate of death 14980 (1961), Charles H. Mason.

10. Mary Mason, *The History and Life Work of Bishop C. H. Mason* (1924; reprint, Memphis: Church of God in Christ, 1987), 19.

11. Jack T. Hunt, *From Prior's Farm to Heaven: Bishop C.H. Mason, A Biography of His Life* (n.p.: Hunt Family Publishing Company, 1995), 6.

12. Calvin White, "In the Beginning, There Stood Two: Arkansas Roots of the Black Holiness Movement," *Arkansas Historical Quarterly* 68, no. 1 (Spring 2009): 1–22. At the time the article was published, White was Assistant Professor of History at University of Arkansas (Fayetteville).

13. See, for example, Al Westbrooks, Jr., "Church of God's Bishop Mason to be Funeralized November 28," *Atlanta Daily World,* 21 November 1961, p. 1, cols. 1–3; "Deaths Elsewhere: Founder of Church," *Washington Post-Times Herald,* 18 November 1961, p. C5, col. 1.

14. Social Security Administration, "Social Security Death Index," database, *Ancestry.com* (http://www.ancestry.com: accessed 30 April 2012), entry for Leila M. Byas, 2004, SS no. not provided.

15. Hunt, *From Prior's Farm to Heaven,* 7–8.

16. Ithiel C. Clemmons, *Bishop C. H. Mason and the Roots of the Church of God in Christ* (Bakersfield, Calif.: Pneuma Life Publishing, 1996), 4.

17. "Genealogical Services," *American Baptist Historical Society* (http://www.abhsarchives.org/services_genealogy.html : accessed March 16, 2012).

18. Kirsten J. Moncada, Social Security Administration, Baltimore, Maryland, to Christopher Brennan, letter, 6 September 2012, response to application for SS-5 of Charles Harrison Mason; Personal Correspondence, 2012; C.H. Mason, Brennan Research Files; privately held by Brennan, Highland Park, New Jersey.

19. Faulkner County, Arkansas, Marriage Record, p. 397, Charles H. Mason and Alice R. Saxton, recorded marriage affidavit; digital image, *Family Search* (https://familysearch.org/pal:/MM9.3.1/

TH-267-12056-181431-60?cc=1417439&wc=14061894 : accessed 8 September 2013); citing FHL microfilm, 1,033,396, item 1.

20. "Louis Armstrong," *Wikipedia* (http://en.wikipedia.org/wiki/Louis_Armstrong : accessed 8 September 2013).

21. United States War Department, *The War of the Rebellion: A Compilation of the Official Records of the Union and Confederate Armies*, ed. Robert N. Scott, et al. (Washington, D.C.: General Printing Office, 1891), series 1, v. 32, part 1, p. 608–609; digital image, *Making of America* (http://ebooks.library.cornell.edu/m/moawar : accessed 16 March 2013).

22. *War of the Rebellion*, 610.

23. Survivors accounts can be found in ibid., series 1, v. 32, part 1, p. 519–40.

24. Ibid., series 1, v. 32, part 1, p. 610.

25. John Cimprich, *Fort Pillow: A Civil War Massacre, and Public Memory* (Baton Rouge: Louisiana University Press, 2005), 129.

26. Ibid.

27. "History of African Americans in the Civil War," *Civil War Soldier and Sailors System, National Park Service* (http://www.itd.nps.gov/cwss/history/aa_history.htm : accessed March 17, 2012).

28. Cimprich, *Fort Pillow*, 127.

29. "United States Colored Troops, 12th Regiment, United States Colored Heavy Artillery," *Civil War Soldiers and Sailors System, National Park Service* (http://www.itd.nps.gov/cwss/soldiers.cfm : accessed March 17, 2012).

30. "United States Colored Troops, 44th Regiment, United States Colored Infantry," *Civil War Soldiers and Sailors System* (http://www.itd.nps.gov/cwss/soldiers.cfm : accessed March 17, 2012).

31. National Archives and Records Administration, U.S., Colored Troops Military Service Records, 1861–1865, *Ancestry.com* (http://www.ancestry.com : accessed March 17, 2012); citing National Archives microfilm publication M1994, roll 66.

32. Letter of Col. William P. Hardeman to Lt. Col. H.A. McCaleb, re: capture of Pvt. Wilson Wood of the 6th U.S. Colored Heavy Artillery, 30 July 1864. National Archives and Records Administration, Compiled Service Records,

Records of the Adjutant General's Office, 1780's–1917, RG 94. See also the discussion of the issue in James McPherson, *Battle Cry of Freedom: The Civil War Era* (New York: Ballantine Books, 1988), 793–96.

33. Walter L. Williams, "Again in Chains: Black Soldiers Suffering in Captivity," *Civil War Times* (May 1981): 40–41; Dudley Taylor Cornish, *The Sable Arm: Negro Troops in the Union Army 1861–1865* (New York: W.W. Norton, 1966), 178.

34. Mason, *The History and Life Work of Bishop C. H. Mason*, 19; Hunt, *From Prior's Farm to Heaven*, 8.

35. "Freedmen's Marriage Certificates, 1865–1869, Roll 2: Tennessee Maas-McDonald," *Freedmen's Bureau Online* (http://freedmensbureau.com/tennessee/marriages/tennmarrm2.htm : accessed March 12, 2012).

36. Reginald Washington, "Sealing the Sacred Bonds of Holy Matrimony," Prologue 37, no. 1 (Spring 2005), digital image, *National Archives and Records Administration* (http://www.archives.gov/publications/prologue/2005/spring/freedman-marriage-recs.html : accessed 4 January 2013).

37. "Freedmen's Marriage Certificates, 1865–1869, Roll 2: Tennessee Maas-McDonald," *Freedmen's Bureau Online.*

38. 1870 U.S. census, Shelby County, Tennessee, population schedule, p. 31 (written), dwelling 216, family 216, Cherry and Eliza Mason; digital image, *Ancestry.com* (http://www.ancestry.com : March 12, 2012); citing National Archives microfilm publication M593, roll 1560.

39. Ibid.

40. Ibid.

41. Mason, *The History and Life Work of Bishop C. H. Mason,* 19.

42. Clemmons, *Bishop C. H. Mason and the Roots of the Church of God in Christ,* 4.

43. 1880 U.S. census, Town of Howard, Arkansas, population schedule, enumeration district (ED) 37, p. 277 (stamped), p. 47 (penned), dwelling 7, family 7, Jeremiah and Eliza Mason; digital image, *Ancestry.com* (http://www.ancestry.com : accessed March 12, 2012); citing National Archives microfilm publication T9, roll 41.

44. Ibid.

45. Frederick Douglass, *Life and Times of Frederick Douglass,* Written by Himself, in the Autobiographies series, notes by Henry Louis Gates, Jr. (New York: Literary Classics of the United States, 1994), 475–76. The text of the Life and Times is a reprint of the edition published in 1893.

46. Booker T. Washington, *Up from Slavery* (New York: Doubleday, 1901), 23; digital text, *American Studies at the University of Virginia,* http://xroads.virginia.edu/~hyper/washington/ch02.html, accessed September 10, 2013). The quote appears in the second paragraph of "Chapter 2, Boyhood Days."

47. "Spotlight: Ruth Randall, CG," *On Board,* 19, no. 2 (May 2013): 24.

48. "List of Persons and Personal Property Assessed for Taxation in Howard County, Arkansas for the Years 1887–1894," Arkansas State Archives (Little Rock, Arkansas), microfilm roll 47.

49. Ibid.

50. 1910 U.S. census, Holmes County, Mississippi, population schedule, ward 1, enumeration district (ED) 42, sheet 3B, dwelling 53, family 59, C.H. Mason; digital image, *Ancestry.com* database, citing NARA microfilm publication T624, roll 742; FHL microfilm 1,374,755.

51. 1920 U.S. census, Shelby County, Tennessee, population schedule, Civil District 7, part of Memphis, enumeration district (ED) 231, sheet

26-A, dwelling 672, family 681, Charles Mason; digital image, *Ancestry.com* (http://www.ancestry.com : April 30, 2012), citing NARA microfilm publication T625, roll 1766.

52. 1930 U.S. census, Shelby County, Tennessee, population schedule, ward 25, block 125, , p. 268 (stamped), Memphis, enumeration district (ED) 79-212, sheet 28A, dwelling 184, family 185, Charles Mason; digital image, *Ancestry.com* (http://www.ancestry.com : April 30, 2012), citing NARA microfilm publication T626; FHL microfilm 2,342,010.

53. "List of Persons and Personal Property Assessed for Taxation in Howard County, Arkansas, for the Years 1887–1894," Arkansas State Archives (Little Rock, Arkansas), microfilm roll 47.

54. Conway County, Arkansas, Eliza Mason will (1897); proof of will, 31 May 1904; Circuit Clerk of Conway County, Arkansas, Morrilton.

55. Hunt, *From Prior's Farm to Heaven*, 12. Hunt seems to think Israel Nelson is the only stepbrother to C.H. Mason. He refers to Israel as J. H. Nelson, but it clear from the context who is meant.

56. Martha Simmons and Frank A. Thomas, *Preaching with Sacred Fire: An Anthology of African American Sermons, 1750 to the Present* (New York: W.W. Norton, 2010), 434.

CHAPTER 3: AFRICAN ROOTS AND MULTICULTURAL MISSION OF AFROPENTECOSTALISM

1. Earlier forms of this chapter were presented at the COGIC Scholar's Academic Forum, Auxiliaries in Ministry, St. Louis, Missouri, July 4, 2001; and at the Society for Pentecostal Studies, Southeastern University, Lakeland, Florida, February 14, 2002. This chapter will be expanded as "Charles Mason's Roots and the Transatlantic Politics of Healing" in *African Roots and Political Dance: Cultural History and Political Arts in Afropentecostal Practice* [working title] (Bloomington, Ind.: Indiana University Press, forthcoming).

2. James Courts, *The History and Life Work of Elder C.H. Mason, Chief Apostle and His Co-Laborers* (n.p., 1920), 15, cited in David Douglas Daniels III, *The Cultural Renewal of Slave Religion: Charles Price Jones and the Emergence of the Holiness Movement in Mississippi* (Ph.D. dissertation, Union Theological Seminary, 1992), 90.

3. Melville J. Herskovits, *The Myth of the Negro Past* (Boston: Beacon Press, 1941).

4. Philip D. Curtin, *The Atlantic Slave Trade* (Madison, Wis.: University of Wisconsin Press, 1969), and George Eaton Simpson, *Black Religions in the New World* (New York: Columbia University Press, 1978).

5. Simpson, *Black Religions in the New World*, 11.

6. Joseph M. Murphy, *Working the Spirit: Ceremonies of the African Diaspora* (Boston: Beacon Press, 1994).

7. Based on a rhetorical Henry Louis Gates, *The Signifying Monkey: A Theory of Afro-American Literary Criticism* (New York: Oxford University Press, 2008).

8. Robert C. Williams also suggests that black history-experience is embodied in the dramas, rituals, and encounters of Black worship in, "Ritual, Drama, and God in Black Religion: Theological and Anthropological Views," *Theology Today* 41, no. 4 (1985):431–43.

9. Jan Vansina, *Paths in the Rainforest: Toward a History of Political Tradition in Equatorial Africa* (Madison, Wis.: University of Wisconsin Press, 1990).

10. Yvonne Bastian, André Coupez, and Michael Mann, *Continuity and Divergence in the Bantu Languages: Perspectives from a Lexicostatistic Study* (Tervuren, Belgium: Musée Royal de l'Afrique Centrale, 1999).

11. Cognates are words that have a common origin (etymology). An example of a cognate in Indo-European languages are the words *night* (English), *nuit* (French), *nacht* (German), *nacht* (Dutch), *nicht* (Scots), *natt* (Swedish, Norwegian), *nat* (Danish), *nátt* (Faroese), *nótt* (Icelandic), *noc* (Czech, Slovak, Polish),...all meaning "night" and derived from the Proto-Indo-European (PIE) *nók^(w)ts, 'night'" (http://en.wikipedia.org/wiki/Cognate, accessed July 1, 2011).

12. See two books by David Lee Schoenbrun, *The Historical Reconstruction of Great Lakes Bantu Cultural Vocabulary: Etymologies and Distributions* (Köln, Germany: Rüdiger Köppe Verlag, 1997), and *A Green Place, a Good Place: Agrarian Change, Gender, and Social Identity in the Great Lakes Region to the 15th Century* (Portsmouth, N.H.: Heinemann, 1998).

13. Jan Vansina, "Comments on Christopher Ehret, 'Bantu History: Re-envisioning the Evidence of Language,'" *International Journal of African Historical Studies* 34, no. 1 (2001): 52.

14. The broad distributions of Bantu languages, along with archeological distributions, confirms development of an ancient African Bantu network of languages, which was accompanied by social and technological trade (see John Janzen, *Lemba 1650–1930: A Drum of Affliction in Africa and the New World* [New York: Garland Publishing, 1982]), often following river routes (see Vansina, *Paths in the Rainforest*, 188).

15. John M. Janzen, *Ngoma Discourses of Healing in Central and Southern Africa* (Berkeley, Calif.: University of California Press, 1992); see also, Allan Anderson, *Zion and Pentecost: The Spirituality and Experience of Pentecostal and Zionist/Apostolic Churches in South Africa* (Pretoria, South Africa: University of South Africa Press, 2000).

16. Janzen, *Ngoma*, 63.

17. Rijk Van Dijk, Ria Reis, and Marja Spierenburg define *ngoma* by three themes that would be recognized by both participants and researchers: "1) ngoma is a way of articulating and commenting on processes of transition or transformation; 2) it produces a certain type of power and authority, which is based on claims to a specific association

and communication with the spirit world; 3) this power is embodied, expressed and effected in rhythm (drumming, singing, dancing)," *The Quest for Fruition Through Ngoma: Political Aspects of Healing in Southern Africa* (Oxford, England: James Currey., 2000), 7.

18. Donald W. Dayton, *Theological Roots of Pentecostalism* (Metuchen, N.J.: Hendrickson Publishers, 1987), 17.

19. Amos Yong has summarized Pentecostal's fivefold gospel as focused in the roles of Jesus as "savior, sanctifier, Spirit-baptizer, healer, and coming king" in his book, *In the Days of Caesar: Pentecostalism and Political Theology* (Grand Rapids, Mich.: Eerdmans, 2009), 95; Yong uses this five-foldness to organize each chapter in part two of the book as he develops a Pentecostal political theology. Regarding the centrality of Jesus as the "coming king" and of eschatology in Pentecostal theology, David W. Faupel has written *The Everlasting Gospel: the Significance of Eschatology in the Development of Pentecostal Thought* (Sheffield, England: Sheffield Academic Press, 1996).

20. Walter J. Hollenweger identifies the black oral root of Pentecostalism and notes parallels between Black Pentecostalism in the United States, South Africa, and Zaïre in *Pentecostalism: Origins and Developments Worldwide* (Peabody, Mass.: Hendrickson Publishers, 1997), 18–141. Hollenweger also identifies, by book sections, Wesleyan-Catholic, Evangelical, Critical, and Ecumenical roots of Pentecostalism.

21. The literature on African rituals and *ngoma* is rich and includes observations from explorers, missionaries, anthropologists, and practitioners. In addition to sources above–Janzen, Ngoma; Van Dijk et. al., *Quest for Fruition Through Ngoma*–other significant works include two addition books by Janzen, *The Quest for Therapy in Lower Zaire* (Berkeley, Calif.: University of California Press, 1978), and *Lemba 1650–1930: A Drum of Affliction in Africa and the New World* (New York: Garland Publishing, 1982); Jean Comaroff, *Body of Power, Spirit of Resistance: The Culture and History of a South African People* (Chicago: University of Chicago Press, 1985); Bengt G. M. Sundkler, *Bantu Prophets in South Africa* (London, England: Lutterworth Press, 1948), and *Zulu Zion and Some Swazi Zionists* (Oxford: Oxford University Press, 1976); and Marthinus Louis Daneel, *Quest for Belonging: Introduction to a Study of African Independent Churches* (Gweru, Zimbabwe : Mambo Press, 1987).

22. Charles H Mason, 1924. *The History and Life Work of Elder C. H. Mason, Chief Apostle and his Co-Laborers.* Edited by Mary Mason (Memphis, TN: Np, 1924).

23. Sherry Sherrod DuPree, *African-American Holiness Pentecostal Movement: An Annotated Bibliography* (New York: Garland Publishing, 1996), photo inset after page 348.

24. Ithiel C. Clemmons, *Bishop C.H. Mason and the Roots of the Church of God in Christ* (Bakersfield, Calif.: Pneuma Life Publishing, 1996), 33–34.

"Mystical wonders of God" quote in Clemmons, 34, is found originally from David Tucker, *Black Pastors and Leaders, Memphis, 1819–1972* (Memphis, Tenn.: Memphis State University Press, 1975), 92.

25. Early missionaries often referred to "*ngangas*" as "witch doctors," but witches use their powers against others and for personal gain, whereas ngangas use their power to reverse the powers of witches and angry ancestors to restore healing and the flow of social and economic wealth to the afflicted and the community.

26. Wyatt MacGaffey and Rene Stout, *Astonishment and Power: The Eyes of Understanding: Kongo Minkisi* (Washington, D.C.: National Gallery of Art, 1993).

27. Ibid., 56, 58, 76.

28. Robert Farris Thompson, *Flash of the Spirit* (New York: Vintage Books, 1983), 131.

29. Moses's staff became a lively snake (Ex. 4:1–5); his cloak became able to cause and heal leprosy; his pouring able to turn water into blood (4:6–9). Aaron's staff became a snake that swallowed the magicians' snakes (7:1–12); and both their staffs were used in Egypt to turn water to blood (7:14–24), cover the land with frogs and locust (8:1–15; 10:1–20), cover bodies with boils (9:8–12), fill the sky with hail and darkness (9:13–35; 10:21–29), and kill the Egyptians' firstborn sons (11:1–12:30). After their exodus, Moses struck a rock with his staff to bring forth needed water, and he put a snake on a pole as an icon for healing (Num. 20:1–11; 21:4–9). And though material influences seemed to be concentrated in these biblical stories of slave liberation, they did not end with Moses: Elisha used water in healing Naaman (2 Kings 5), Jesus used spittle and mud to give sight to a blind man (Mk. 8:23), Christians in Ephesus used handkerchiefs that had touched Paul to heal (Acts 19:12), and James instructed elders to use hands and olive oil with righteous prayer to heal the sick (Jas. 5:14). The Bible also describes (for example): protective amulets prescribed as protection against evil (Deut. 6:4–9; 11:18–21); invocations and ritual prescriptions for military victory (Ex. 17:8–16; Judg. 7); acts of obedience as conditions of blessings, and of disobedience as conditions of curses (Deut. 11:26–32); a chest of sacred objects used to effect blessings (Deut. 10:8); control of weather for conditions favorable to farming, warfare, transportation (Deut. 10:13–15; Josh. 4:12–14; Mt. 8:26); substances changed from one thing to another (Jn. 2:4–10); prayers made to multiply food for a crowd (Mt. 14:15–21); an unfruitful fig tree cursed and withered (Mt. 21:19); nine people raised from the dead–from Elijah through Jesus to Dorcas (1 Kings 17:17–22; Mt. 28:5–8; Acts 9:36–42); numerous healings (Gen. 20:17); and many dreams interpreted as divine signs or directives (Gen. 40).

30. Personal Interview with David Daniels, III, Tulsa, Okla., March 10, 2001.

31. Charles Mason in J.O. Patterson, German R. Ross, and Julia Mason Atkins, *History and Formative Years of the Church of God in Christ with Excerpts from the Life and Work of its Founder–Bishop C. H. Mason* (Memphis: Church of God in Christ Publishing House, 1969), 36.

32. Ibid.

33. Note that Jesus' Great Commission included *both* ritual and didactic methods: "make disciples by baptizing…and teaching…" (Mt. 28:19–20).

34. *History and Formative Years.*

35. Ibid.

36. Evelyn Brooks Higginbotham, *Righteous Discontent: The Women's Movement in the Black Baptist Church 1880–1920* (Cambridge, Mass.: Harvard University Press, 1993).

37. David Douglass Daniels, *The Cultural Renewal of Slave Religion: Charles Price Jones and the Emergence of the Holiness Movement in Mississippi* (Ph.D. Diss., Union Theological Seminary, 1992), and "African-American Pentecostalism in the 20th Century," in *The Century of the Holy Spirit: 100 Years of Pentecostal and Charismatic Renewal, 1901–2001*, ed. Vinson Synan (Nashville: Thomas Nelson Publishers, 2001); Walter J. Hollenweger, *Pentecostalism: Origins and Developments Worldwide* (Peabody, Mass.: Hendrickson Publishers, 1997), and "The Black Roots of Pentecostalism," in *Pentecostals after a Century*, ed. Allan H. Anderson and Walter J. Hollenweger (Sheffield, England: Sheffield Academic Press, 1999); Leonard Lovett, "Black Origins of the Pentecostal Movement," in *Aspects of Pentecostal-Charismatic Origins*, ed. Vinson Synan (Plainfield, N.J.: Logos International, 1975); idem., *Black Holiness-Pentecostalism: Implications for Ethics and Social Transformation* (Ph.D. Diss., Emory, 1978) and "Aspects of the Spiritual Legacy of the Church of God in Christ: Ecumenical Implications," *Mid-Stream* 24, no. 4 (1985): 389–97, also in *Black Witness to Apostolic Faith*, ed. David T. Shannon and Gayraud S. Wilmore (Grand Rapids, Mich.: Eerdmans, 1985); Arthur E. Paris, *Black Pentecostalism: Southern Religion in an Urban World* (Amherst, Mass.: University of Massachusetts Press, 1982); Thomasina Neely, Belief, *Ritual and Performance in a Black Pentecostal Church: The Musical Heritage of the Church of God in Christ* (Ph.D. Diss. Bloomington, Ind.: Indiana University, 1993); James S. Tinney, "Black Origins of the Pentecostal Movement," *Christianity Today* (October 8, 1971): 4–6; idem., "Black Pentecostals: Setting Up the Kingdom," *Christianity Today* (December 5, 1975):278–79; idem., *A Theoretical and Historical Comparison of Black Political and Religious Movements* (Ph.D. Diss., Howard, 1978); idem.,"The Blackness of Pentecostalism," *Spirit: A Journal of Issues Incident to Black Pentecostalism* 3, no. 2 (1979): 27–36.

I have identified Holiness camp meetings at a cultural-ritual space for developing Christian Africanicity. See chapter five, "Reconstruction and the Performative Politics of Holiness," in Scandrett-Leatherman, *African Roots and Political Dance: Cultural History and Political Arts in Afropentecostal*

Practice [working title] (Bloomington, Ind.: Indiana University Press, forthcoming).

38. Robert Franklin, quoted in Joe Maxwell, "Building the Church (of God in Christ)," *Christianity Today* (April 8, 1996): 22–28.

39. Lamin Sanneh, *Translating the Message: The Missionary Impact on Culture* (Maryknoll, N.Y.; Orbis Books, 1989).

40. W.E. Burghardt Du Bois, *The Souls of Black Folk* (New York: Signet, 1905).

41. Michelle Alexander, *The New Jim Crow: Mass Incarceration in the Age of Colorblindness* (New York: New Press, 2010).

42. Melvin L. Oliver and Thomas M. Shapiro, *Black Wealth/White Wealth: A New Perspective on Racial Inequality* (London, England: Routledge, 2006).

43. David Douglass Daniels, III, "'Everybody Bids You Welcome': A Multicultural Approach to North American Pentecostalism," in *The Globalization of Pentecostalism: A Religion Made to Travel*, ed. Murray W. Dempster, Byron D. Klaus, and Douglas Peterson (Irvine, Calif.: Renum Books, 1999).

44. C. René Padilla, "The Unity of the Church and the Homogeneous Unit Principle," in *Exploring Church Growth*, ed. Wilbert R. Shenk (Grand Rapids, Mich.: William B. Eerdmans, 1983), 291.

45. Moss quoted in Timothy M. Kalil, "Thomas A. Dorsey and the Development and Diffusion of Traditional Black Gospel Piano," in *Perspectives on American Music, 1900–1950*, ed. Michael Saffle (New York: Garland, 2000), 174.

46. Evelyn Ch'ien, "Creative Technology and Rap," *World Englishes* 30, no. 1 (2011): 60–75.

47. Paul Oliver, *Songsters and Saints: Vocal Traditions on Race Records* (Cambridge, Mass.: Cambridge University Press, 1984), 172.

48. Sandra L. Barnes, "Religion and Rap Music: An Analysis of Black Church Usage," *Review of Religious Research* 49, no. 3 (2008): 326–28.

49. Ibid., 328, 332.

50. Horace Clarence Boyer, *How Sweet the Sound: The Golden Age of Gospel* (Washington, D.C.: Elliott & Clark Publishing, 1995). Lynn Abbott, *I Got Two Wings: Incidents and Anecdotes of the Two-Winged Preacher and Electric Guitar Evangelist, Elder Utah Smith* (Brooklyn, N.Y.: CaseQuarter, 2008).

51. Timothy M .Kalil, "Thomas A. Dorsey and the Development and Diffusion of Traditional Black Gospel Piano," Ed. Michael Saffle, *Perspectives on American Music, 1900-1950* (New York: Garland, 2000), 174.; Evelyn Ch'ien, "Creative Technology and Rap," *World Englishes* 30, no. 1 (2011):60-75.; Paul Oliver, *Songsters and Saints: Vocal Traditions on Race Records* (Cambridge, MA: Cambridge University Press, 1984), 172.; Sandra L. Barnes, "Religion and Rap Music: An Analysis of Black Church Usage,"

Review of Religious Research 49, no. 3 (2008):326-28.; Barnes, "Religion and Rap," 328, 332.; Horace Clarence Boyer, *How Sweet the Sound: The Golden Age of Gospel* (Washington, D.C.: Elliott & Clark Publishing, 1995). Lynn Abbott, *I Got Two Wings: Incidents and Anecdotes of the Two-Winged Preacher and Electric Guitar Evangelist, Elder Utah Smith* (Brooklyn, NY: CaseQuarter, 2008).; Patricia Harkins-Pierre, "Religion Bridge: Translating Secular Music into Sacred Music: A Study of World Christianity Focusing on the U.S. Virgin Islands," in *The Changing Face of Christianity: Africa, the West, and the World*, ed. Lamin Sanneh and Joel A. Carpenter (New York: Oxford University Press, 2005), 21–44. Teresa Reed, *The Holy Profane: Religion in Black Popular Music* (Lexington, Ky.: University of Kentucky Press, 2003).

52. See Don Cusic, *The Sound of Light: The History of Gospel Music* (Bowling Green, Ohio: Bowling Green State University Popular Press, 1990), and Michael W. Harris, *The Rise of Gospel Blues: The Music of Thomas Andrew Dorsey in the Urban Church* (New York: Oxford University Press, 1992).

CHAPTER 4: CHARLES HARRISON MASON AS SIGN READER AND INTERPRETER

1. In Figure 1, Bishop Charles Harrison Mason poses with unusually formed objects used as illustrations in his sermons. The photograph appears in Larry G. Britton,ed., *A Memphis Corporate Salute: Bishop Charles Harrison Mason, Founder of Church of God in Christ* (Mempis: Church of God in Christ Public Relations Department, 1994): 29, and Lucille Cornelius, *The History of the Church of God in Christ* (n.p., 1975): 14.

2. *Webster's Revised Unabridged Dictionary*, 1913, s.v., "Signs." This is a use of the term that may have been, early in the twentieth century, standard for Mason and other persons.

3. Paul Tillich, "Religious Symbols and Our Knowledge of God," *The Christian Scholar* 38, no. 3 (September 1955): 189–97.

4. Mary Mason, *The History and Life Work of Elder C.H. Mason, Chief Apostle, and His Co-Laborers* (Memphis: Church of God in Christ Publishing House, 1987).

5. Symbolic language is ultimately a group process. Tillich points out that while individuals can be creative in constructing signs and symbols, the social group must first recognize and consent to the representational use of the object or event in order for either to become a genuine sign or symbol. Tillich, 192.

6. "Church Celebrates 50th Anniversary," *Ebony* (March 1958): 58, quoted in David Tucker's *Black Pastors and Leaders: Memphis, 1819–1972* (Memphis: Memphis State Univ. Press, 1975).

7. This news article was relayed by wire and printed in the *Los Angeles Times*, July 3, 1914, I9.

8. That Mason would have snakelike shapes in his collection reflects the snake's large role in the system of signs in folk culture. See Newbell Niles Puckett, *Folk Beliefs of the Southern Negro* (Chapel Hill, N.C.: University of North Carolina Press, 1968), 321–22.

9. The reporter is unaware of or does not acknowledge the use of vegetables beyond their consumption as food. Irish and sweet potatoes were used in folk culture for conjure and healing practices, and various signs in weather-lore determined when potatoes would be planted and harvested. See Ibid., 223, 315, 350, 360, 365, 388.

10. Mason, *History and Life Work*, 30

11. Ibid., 30

12. Cheryl J. Sanders, *Saints in Exile: The Holiness-Pentecostal Experience in African American Religion and Culture* (New York: Oxford University Press, 1996), 29.

13. C. Eric Lincoln and Lawrence H. Mamiya, *The Black Church in the African American Experience* (Durham, N.C.: Duke University Press, 1990), 90.

14. U.S. Department of Commerce, *We the Americans: Blacks* (Washington, D.C.: Government Printing Office, September 1993), 2.

15. U.S. Department of Commerce, *Population Change and Distribution: 1990 to 2000* [C2KBR/01-2]. Table 2: "Population Change and 2000 Share by Metropolitan Status and Size Category: 1990 to 2000" (Washington, D.C.: Government Printing Office, April 2001), 5

16. U.S. Department of Commerce, *The Black Population in the United States: March 2002.* Figure 2: "Metropolitan and Nonmetropolitan Residence by Race: 2002," (Washington, D.C.: Government Printing Office, April 2001), 2.

17. Ibid., 1.

18. Andrew F. Frank, *The Routledge Historical Atlas of the American South* (New York: Routledge, 1999), 95.

19. Some biographers set the year of Mason's birth as early as 1863. See Lelia Mason Byas, *"The Life and Times of Bishop C.H. Mason"* [audio recording], produced by the Historical Cultural Museum and Fine Arts Center, Church of God in Christ (Memphis: Church of God in Christ Publishing House, 1987).and Cornelius, History, 16.

20. Ithiel C. Clemmons, *Bishop C.H. Mason and the Roots of the Church of God in Christ* (Bakersfield, Calif.: Pneuma Life Publishing, 1996), 4.

21. Byas, *Life and Times* recording.

22. Clemmons, *Bishop C.H. Mason*, 5–6, 8–15.

23. Ibid., 64–65.

24. Ibid., 66.

25. Charles Wilson Reagan and William Ferris, eds., *Encyclopedia of Southern Culture* (Chapel Hill, N.C.: University of North Carolina Press, 1987), 319.

26. Ibid., 32.
27. Ibid., 34.
28. Ibid., 361–62.
29. Ibid., 135.
30. Ibid., 135.
31. Hans A. Baer and Merrill Singer classify Pentecostal denominations as conversionist sects that tend to deal with social problems apolitically, recommending that their members separate themselves from society and follow a strict moral life. Conversionist sects provide their members with an emotional release from the pressure and hardship of oppression through expressive acts, such as shouting, dancing, speaking in tongues, and other manifestations of the sanctified life. See their "Toward a Typology of Black Sectarianism as a Response to Racial Stratification," in *African-American Religion: Interpretive Essays in History and Culture*, ed. Timothy E. Fulop and Albert J. Raboteau (New York: Routledge, 1997), 258–76. They render a more extensive treatment and contrast and comparison of religious strategies for dealing with social problems in their *African-American Religion: Varieties of Protest and Accommodation* (Knoxville, Tenn.: University of Tennessee Press, 2002).
32. Lawrence W Levine, *Black Culture and Black Consciousness: Afro-American Folk Thought from Slavery to Freedom* (New York: Oxford University Press, 1978), 66.
33. Puckett, *Folk Beliefs of the Southern Negro*, 311.
34. Ibid., 312.
35. Levine, *Black Culture and Black Consciousness*, 68, 78.
36. Puckett, *Folk Beliefs of the Southern Negro*, 519.
37. Ibid., 313.
38. Ibid.
39. The multiple influences–African, European, and Native American–that shape Black folk culture are cited in Newbell Niles Puckett's *Folk Beliefs of the Southern Negro*, 78; Lawrence W. Levine's *Black Culture and Black Consciousness*, 60; and Yvonne Chireau's *Black Magic* (Berkeley: Univ. of California Press, 2003): 55–57. For more extensive study of the myriad of racial and ethnic influences, especially Native American, upon the formation of black cultural life, see Patrick Neal Minges's *Slavery in the Cherokee Nation: The Keetoowah Society and the Defining of a People, 1855-1867* (New York, NY: Routledge, 2003) and *Black Indian Slave Narratives* (Winston Salem, NC: John F. Blair Publisher, 2004), and Jack D. Forbes's *Africans and Native Americans: The Language of Race and the Evolution of Red-Black Peoples* (Chicago: University of Illinois Press, 1993).
40. Levine, *Black Culture and Black Consciousness*, 58.
41. Ibid., 66.
42. John Mason Brewer, *American Negro Folklore* (Chicago: Quadrangle Books, 1968), 287.

43. John S. Mbiti, *African Religions and Philosophy* (Garden City, N.Y.: Doubleday, 1970), 67–74.

44. Puckett, *Folk Beliefs of the Southern Negro*, 171–72.

45. Mbiti, *African Religions and Philosophy*, 89.

46. Ibid., 231-233.

47. Ibid., 60–61, 267, 269, 274.

48. Levine, *Black Culture and Black Consciousness*, 57. Henry H. Mitchell, *Black Preaching* (New York: J.B. Lippincott Company, 1970), 53.

49. Zora Neale Hurston, *The Sanctified Church* (New York: Marlowe & Company, 1981), 85–86.

50. Levine, *Black Culture and Black Consciousness*, 57.

51. C.G. Brown claims that Mason saw God in everything. In addition to objects and events in nature, Mason would render interpretations of man-made objects. For example, he described a cleaver as (1) the word of God, preached by ministers, (2) God's battle-axe, and (3) a word of condemnation for wicked persons but a word resulting in blessings and no harm to righteous persons who respect the power of the word. Mason, *History and Life Work*, 45.

52. Ibid., 19

53. J. Rodman Williams, *Renewal Theology: Systematic Theology from a Charismatic Perspective* (Grand Rapids, Mich.: Zondervan, 1996), 317–84.

54. Elsie W. Mason, ed., *The Man, Charles Harrison Mason: 1866–1961* (Memphis: Church of God in Christ Publishing House, 1979), 29.

55. Ibid., 32.

56. Mary Mason, *History and Life Work*, 45.

57. Ibid., 92; Elsie W. Mason, *The Man*, 30.

58. H. Richard Niebuhr, *Christ and Culture* (London, England: Faber & Faber Limited, 1952), 154–55, 163–70, 187–91.

59. Weather lore constitutes a substantial portion of beliefs about signs. Puckett, *Folk Beliefs of the Southern Negro*, 505–19; Elsie W. Mason, *The Man*, 22.

60. Ibid., 22.

61. Ibid.

62. Ibid., 23.

63. Elsie W. Mason, *The Man*, 23.

64. Ibid., 31.

65. Mary Mason, *History and Life Work*, 84.

66. Elsie W. Mason, *The Man*, 23.

67. Ibid., 22.

68. Mary Mason, *History and Life Work*, 50.

69. Here "entrails" might refer to the gizzard, an internal organ in the abdominal area or the external growth on the throat of a bird. The chicken's gizzard is used in conjure and healing practices. Puckett, *Folk Beliefs of the Southern Negro*, 223, 240, 298; Mary Mason, *History and Life Work*, 73.

70. The use of roots is central and very extensive in conjure and healing traditions. Puckett, *Folk Beliefs of the Southern Negro,* 222, 230, 245–46, 265–66, 276–77, 280, 292, 298, 300, 331, 341, 346, 364, 366, 376, 383–85, 558.

71. In Figure 2, Mason holds a wooden object in the shape of an animal skull. The photograph appears in Coffey, Lillian Brooks, comp. [1926], *1926 Year Book of the Church of God in Christ.* Material from 1934 Year Book and other Church of God in Christ Publications added by Jerry R. Ramsey. Memphis: Church of God in Christ, 1991: title page.

72. Figure 3, a potato resembling a human figure, appears in J.O. Patterson, G.R. Ross, and J.M. Atkins, eds., *History and the Formative Years of the Church of God in Christ* (Memphis: Church of God in Christ Publishing House, 1969), x, and Mary Mason, *History and Life Work,* 15.

73. Elsie W. Mason, *The Man,* 30.

74. In folk culture, Puckett discovered that the bloom and death of trees were regarded as signs. See Puckett, *Folk Beliefs of the Southern Negro,* 493–94. Figure 4, a wooden object resembling a human hand, appears in Patterson, et al., *History and the Formative Years,* xii, and Mary Mason, *History and Life Work,* 17.

75. Mary Mason, *History and Life Work*, 94–95.

76.Lillian Brooks Coffey, comp., *1926 Year Book of the Church of God in Christ.* Material from 1934 Year Book and other Church of God in Christ Publications added by Jerry R. Ramsey (Memphis: Church of God in Christ, 1991), 8.

77. Figure 5, a wooden object resembling a dog with three legs only, appears in Coffey, *1926 Year Book,* 8.

78. Ibid., 8; See also Otis G. Clark, comp., *The Azusa Mission: The Greatest Pentecostal Outpouring Ever Known in the United States* (Oakland, Calif.: 1984), 13.

79. In Black folklore, the dog is a despicable animal that is susceptible of lurking spirits, especially the spirit of death. See Puckett, *Folk Beliefs of the Southern Negro,* 35, 478–79; Elsie W. Mason, *The Man,* 26–27.

80. Mary Mason, *History and Life Work,* 93.

81. Ibid., 93.

82. Elsie W. Mason, *The Man,* 31.

83. Numerous works examine the art of preaching among African Americans. Included among these works are: William H. Pipes, *Say Amen, Brother!: Old Time Negro Preaching* (1951); Henry H. Mitchell, *Black Preaching* (1970) and *The Recovery of Preaching* (1977); Lyndrey A. Niles, "Rhetorical Characteristics of Traditional Black Preaching," *Journal of Black Studies* 15, no. 1 (Sept. 1984): 41–52; Gerald Davis, *I Got the Word in Me and I Can Sing It, You Know: A Study of the Performed African American Sermon* (1985); Jon Michael Spencer, *Sacred Symphony: The Chanted Sermon of the Black Preacher* (1987); Bruce A. Rosenburg, *Can These Bones Live?: The Art of the American Folk Preacher* (1988); William C. Turner, "The Musicality of

Black Preaching: A Phenomenology," *Journal of Black Sacred Music* 2, no. 1 (Spring 1988): 21–34; Evans E. Crawford, *The Hum: Call and Response in African American Preaching* (1995); Frank A. Thomas, *They Never Like to Quit Praisin' God: The Role of Celebration in Preaching* (1997); and L. Susan Bond, *Contemporary African American Preaching: Diversity in Theory and Style* (2003). Collections of sermons, in written form, include: *Best Black Sermons* (1972), ed. William M. Philpot; *Outstanding Black Sermons,* Volumes 1–4 (1976–), ed. J. Alfred Smith, et al.; *Those Preaching Women: Sermons by Black Women Preachers,* Volumes 1–3 (1985–), ed. Ella Pearson Mitchell; and *Daughters of Thunder: Black Women Preachers and Their Sermons, 1850–1970* (c. 1998), ed. Bettye Collier-Thomas.

CHAPTER 5: BISHOP CHARLES HARRISON MASON

1. I.C. Clemmons, *Bishop C.H. Mason and the Roots of the Church of God in Christ* (Bakersfield, Calif.: Pnuema Life Publishing, 1996), 5; Mary Mason, *The History and Life Work of Elder C. H. Mason* (Memphis: Church of God in Christ Publishing, 1987), 23–24; J.O. Patterson, G.R. Ross, and J.M. Atkins, eds., *History and the Formative Years of the Church of God in Christ* (Memphis: Church of God in Christ Publishing House, 1969), 15–16.

2. Clemmons, *Bishop C.H. Mason,* 13; C.H. Pleas, *Fifty Years Achievement from 1906 to 1956: A Period of History of the Church of God in Christ* (Memphis: COGIC Publishing, 1991), 1.

3. Vinson Synan, *The Holiness-Pentecostal Tradition: Charismatic Movements in the Twentieth Century* (Grand Rapids, Mich.: William B. Eerdmans Publishers.) 169.

4. Clemmons, *Bishop C.H. Mason,* 13.

5. Ibid., 8–9.

6. Ibid., 11, 124; O.B. Cobbins, *History of Church of Christ* (Holiness) U.S.A. 1895–1965 (New York: Vantage Press, 1966), 431; Patterson et al., *History and the Formative Years,* 63; *The Official Manual of the Church of God in Christ* (Memphis: COGIC Publishing House, 1973), xxvi.

7. Cobbins, *History of Church of Christ,* 431.

8. Cobbins, *History of Church of Christ,* 28; Pleas, *Fifty Years Achievement,* 6.

9. Cobbins, *History of Church of Christ,* 431; Pleas, *Fifty Years Achievement,* 6–7; *Official Manual of the Church of God in Christ,* xxvi.

10. S.M. Burgess, G.B. McGee, and P.H. Alexander, P. H., eds., *Dictionary of Pentecostal and Charismatic Movements* (Grand Rapids, Mich.: Zondervan Publishing House, 1988), 660; Mason, *History and Life Work,* 26–30; Synan, *The Holiness-Pentecostal Tradition,* 91.

11. Clemmons, *Bishop C.H. Mason,* 64; Synan, *The Holiness-Pentecostal Tradition,* 125; R. Morring, *Mason Memorial Church of God in Christ: 90th Church Anniversary* (Norfolk, Va.: Mason Memorial COGIC, 1996), 17.

12. J. Williams, *The Church That Jesus Builds: A Historical Perspective, 85th Church Anniversary Mason Memorial Church of God in Christ* (n.p., 1991), 23.
13. Ibid., 23.
14. Ibid., 23.
15. Myron Noble, ed., *Like as of Fire* (Washington, D.C.: Middle Atlantic Regional Press, 1985), 7.
16. Clemmons, *Bishop C.H. Mason*, 64.
17. Synan, *The Holiness-Pentecostal Tradition*, 125.
18. Williams, *Church That Jesus Builds*, 23; C. Young, *Special Editorial, 85th Church Anniversary of Mason Memorial Church of God in Christ* (n.p., 1991), 14.
19. Williams, *Church That Jesus Builds*, 23.
20. Clemmons, *Bishop C.H. Mason*, 64; Vinson Synan, "The Quiet Rise of Black Pentecostals," *Charisma*, June 1986, 45–48.
21. Alferd Z. Hall Jr., *So You Want to Know Your Church?* (Memphis: Zannju Publishing. 1995), 12.
22. Clemmons, *Bishop C.H. Mason*, 65; Cobbins, *History of Church of Christ*, 432–33.
23. Clemmons, *Bishop C.H. Mason*, 65.
24. Cobbins, *History of Church of Christ*, 432; Hall, *So You Want to Know*, 12; Synan, *The Holiness-Pentecostal Tradition*, 126.
25. Cobbins, *History of Church of Christ*, 432; Clemmons, *Bishop C.H. Mason*, 65.
26. Clemmons, *Bishop C.H. Mason*, 65.
27. *The Official Manual of the Church of God in Christ*, xxix.
28. Synan, *The Holiness-Pentecostal Tradition*, 126.
29. *The Official Manual of the Church of God in Christ*, 58.
30. Clemmons, *Bishop C.H. Mason*, 66; Cobbins, *History of Church of Christ*, 433.
31. See article in *The Whole Truth*, April 1968, 6.
32. Cobbins, *History of Church of Christ*, 30, 435; Clemmons, *Bishop C.H. Mason*, 66.
33. For further information on slave religion see David D. Daniels III, "The Cultural Renewal of Slave Religion: Charles Price Jones and the Emergence of the Holiness Movement in Mississippi" (Ph.D. dissertation, Union Theological Seminary, 1992).
34. Clemmons, *Bishop C.H. Mason*, 34–35; Synan, *The Holiness-Pentecostal Tradition*, 126.
35. Clemmons, *Bishop C.H. Mason*, 70.
36. R.R. Owens, *Speak to the Rock* (Lanham, Md.: The University Press of America, 1998), 105.
37. Synan, *The Holiness-Pentecostal Tradition*, 171.
38. Owens, *Speak to the Rock*, 85.
39. Clemmons, *Bishop C.H. Mason*, 71.

40. Ibid., 70.
41. Synan, *The Holiness-Pentecostal Tradition*, 171.
42. Burgess, *Dictionary of Pentecostal*, 587.
43. Ibid.
44. Ibid.
45. R. M. Anderson, *Vision of the Disinherited* (Peabody, Mass.: Hendrickson Publishers, 1992), 189.
46. Ibid.
47. J. Maxwell, "Building the Church of God in Christ," *Christianity Today* 40, no. 4 (April 8, 1996): 5.
48. Clemmons, *Bishop C.H. Mason*, 70–71.
49. Ibid., 36–37.
50. Synan, *The Holiness-Pentecostal Tradition*, 155.
51. Burgess, *Dictionary of Pentecostal*, 587.
52. Clemmons, *Bishop C.H. Mason*, 126.

CHAPTER 6: THE CHURCH OF GOD IN CHRIST TRANSFORMS WOMEN'S MINISTRIES THROUGH POSITIVE INFLUENCE OF CHIEF APOSTLE CHARLES HARRISON MASON

1. According to COGIC.org, in 2013 the predominantly African American Church of God in Christ, with a total of more than six million members, is the largest Pentecostal denomination in the United States.
2. Ithiel Clemmons, *Bishop C.H. Mason and the Roots of the Church of God in Christ* (Bakersfield, Calif.: Pneuma Life Publishing,), 67.
3. Anthea Butler, *Women in the COGIC: Making a Sanctified World* (Chapel Hill, N.C.: The University of North Carolina Press, 2007), 37.
4. Cheryl J. Sanders. "History of Women in the Pentecostal Movement," *CYBERJOURNAL FOR PENTECOSTAL-CHARISMATIC RESEARCH*, 1996 PCCNA National Conference, Memphis, Tennessee, October 1, 1996. See http://www.pctii.org/cyberj/cyberj2/SANDERS.pdf.
5. Clemmons, *Pastor C.H. Mason*, 67.
6. Mary Loden, *Implementing Diversity* (Boston: McGraw Hill, 1996).
7. Christine A. Lunardini, *From Equal Suffrage to Equal Rights: Alice Paul and the National Woman's Party, 1910–1928* (New York: New York University Press, 1986), 21–22.
8. Marjorie Spruill Wheeler, *Votes For Women* (Knoxville, Tenn.: University of Tennessee Press, 1995), 77.
9. Adrienne M. Israel and Goldie F. Wells, *Women in Ministry in the Church of God in Christ Student Guide* (Memphis: Church of God in Christ Publishing House, 2002), 9. (In early documents, dated in the 1920s, Mother Robinson's name is spelled Roberson. In documents dated in the 1950s, her name is spelled Robinson. The International Women's Department has determined that the correct spelling is Robinson.)

10. Internet Timeline of African American History 1881–1900 adopted from Lerone Bennett's *Before the Mayflower* (Chicago: Johnson Publishing Co., 1982), W. Augustus Low and Virgil A. *Clift's Encyclopedia of Black America* (New York: Da Capo Press, 1984), and Harry A. Ploski and Warren Marr's *The Negro Almanac* (New York: Bellwether Co., 1976).

11. Ibid.

12. Clemmons, *Bishop C.H. Mason*, 1.

13. Ibid., 46.

14. Glenda Williams Goodson, "Church of God in Christ Women Impacting the Nations through International Missionary Work," *International Journal of Pentecostal Missiology*, vol. 3, 2014.

15. Clemmons, *Bishop C.H. Mason*, 103.

16. Ibid., 105–107.

17. Ibid., 4.

18. Romans 16:1.

19. Butler, *Women in the COGIC*, 41.

20. Ibid., 15.

21. Ibid., 30–31.

22. See http://www.cogic.org/womensdepartment/general-supervisor/past-leaders/.

23. A.T. Moore, *Celebrating the Homegoing of Our Founder Bishop C.H. Mason*, Recorded live at Mason Temple November 28, 1961 (Austin Moore for Altmo Productions, LLC, 2007), Disc 2.

24. Butler, *Women in the COGIC*, 41.

25. ibid, 42.

26. Quoted in "Souvenir Journal," 55th Annual Convention, Churches of God in Christ National and International, November 25–December 7, 1962, Memphis, Tenn., 19.

27. Estrelda Alexander, *Black Fire: One Hundred Years of African American Pentecostalism* (Downers Grove, Ill.: InterVarsity Press 2011), 311.

28. Church of God in Christ, *50 years of progress in California*, 41.

29. Clemmons, *Bishop C.H. Mason*, 116.

30. Ibid, 115.

31. "Souvenir Program," Women's International Convention, Oakland, Calif., 1961, 8–9.

32. Butler, *Women in the COGIC*, 56.

33. *Souvenir Journal, 55th Annual Convention*, 33.

34. Ibid.

35. Ibid.

36. *The Whole Truth, Heritage Series*, Volume XXXII, No. VIII, Memphis, Tenn., Convocation Editor November–December 1994, p. 3, reports that the new auxiliaries included the Young Women's Christian Council, Young People's Willing Workers Chairladies Unit , Light Burners of Africa, Volunteers, District Missionaries Unit, Hospitality Group, Ushers Unit,

Editors and Publishers Unit, Religious Education Club, Ministers' Wives Circle, Bishops' Wives Circle, Stewardess Board, Church Mothers' Unit, National Evangelists Unit, Secretaries Unit, Huldah Club; The Whole Truth Heritage Series, Volume VIII, No. IV, Memphis, Tenn., April 1975,

37. *History of the Church of God in Christ in Illinois*, International Women's Convention, COGIC, Chicago, May 5–9, 1954, p. 14.

38. Albertha McKenzie, ed., *Souvenir Book, Women's International Convention, 1963*, Chicago, History of The COGIC in Illinois, 31.

39. Lillian Brooks Coffey, "Tribute to Bishop C.H. Mason, April 1951 A.D.," *Souvenir Journal, 1st National Convention of the Women of the Church of God in Christ International*, Los Angeles April 25–29, 1951, San Francisco May 1–3, 1951, 2.

40. "International Women's Convention Celebrates 25 years," *The Whole Truth*, Vol. VIII, no. IV, April 1975, Memphis, Tenn., 1.

41. Glenda Williams Goodson, *Royalty Unveiled: Women Trailblazers in C.O.G.I.C. International Missions 1920–1970* (Lancaster, Tex.: HCM Publishing, 2011), 193.

42. Elder Robert E. Roberts, General Secretary Northern Illinois, "Dedicated to Initial Meeting Women's Convention," *Souvenir Journal, 1st National Convention of the Women of the Churches of God in Christ International*, Los Angeles April 25–29, 1951, San Francisco May 1–3, 1951, 1.

43. Luella Westbrook, *The 1953 Post Convention Delegation Tour*, 9.

44. *Souvenir Journal, International Women's Convention, Church of God in Christ*, Chicago, Illinois May 5t–9t, 1954, 9.

45. *History of the Lillian Brooks Coffey Rest Home*, 5, 7, 34. Available online on the website of University of Southern California digital library.

46. *Church of God in Christ Official Manual*, 1973, 1991, 1992. According to the manual, Mason appointed seven men "to assist him with resolving grave grievances within jurisdictions, and other related business affairs." It was later known as the Executive Commission. The names of the seven men on the Executive Commission, and the dates of their appointment, are as follows: Bishop A.B. McEwen (6/5/51); Bishop J.D. Bailey (6/5/51); Bishop O.M. Kelly (6/5/51); Bishop J.O. Patterson (5/19/52), Bishop U.E. Miller, S.M. Crouch, and O.T. Jones (10/12/55). Three of the men would serve on the church's first General Board, with Patterson becoming the first elected Presiding Bishop in 1968, xxx–xxxiii.

47. "Eras in Black History," *The Encyclopedia Britannica Guide to Black History*, http://blackhistory.eb.com/

48. *The Whole Truth*, Vol. XXXII, no. VIII, Convocation Edition November–December 1994, Memphis, Tenn., "The Heritage Series," 3.

49. Ibid.

50. Ibid.

51. During the late nineteen and early twentieth century, state normal schools welcomed women, minorities, and other atypical students and

encouraged them to reach beyond their underprivileged backgrounds. Colored normal schools curriculum included preparation and training of teachers, the arts and sciences, home economics, agriculture, and mechanical arts. Tuskegee Institute (Tuskegee University), led by Booker T. Washington, was a famous normal school.

52. Quoted by Moore, *Celebrating the Homegoing*, Disk 2.

53. Butler, *Women in the COGIC*, 110.

54. Mayme O.Brown, "Mississippi Mud," *The Crisis* (May 1936): 142.

55. Glenda Williams Goodson, *Bishop C.H. Mason and Those Sanctified Women!* (Lancaster, Tex.: HCM Publishing 2002), 32.

56. *Souvenir Program, 57th Annual Convention, Churches of God in Christ National and International*, November 25–December 10, 1964, Mason Temple, Memphis, Tenn., 35

57. *Souvenir Program, 66th Annual Holy Convocation*, November 6–16, 1973, 938 Mason Street, Memphis, Tenn., 31

58. Clayborne Carson, ed., *The Papers of Martin Luther King, Jr.: Birth of a New Age: December 1955–December 1956 by Martin Luther King*, vol. 3 (Berkley and Los Angeles, Calif.: University of California Press, 1997), 51. Dexter Avenue Baptist Church was the center of the 1955–1956 Montgomery Bus boycott and Mallory's speaking engagement is significant because of the courage she exhibited in supporting the beginning of the modern civil rights movement.

59. *Souvenir Program, 66th Annual Holy Convocation*, November 6–16, 1973, 938 Mason St., Memphis, Tenn., 31

60. Cora Agnes Berry, quoted in Glenda Williams Goodson, *I'm So Glad I'm Sanctified! Wisdom Quotes and Treasures from C.O.G.I.C. Pioneering Women 1911–1975* (Lancaster, Tex.: HCM Publishing, 2005), 21.

61. *The Whole Truth*, Vol. XXXIII, no. VI, COGIC Headquarters, Memphis, Tenn., July 1995, 3.

62. *Souvenir Program, 48th National Convocation C.O.G.I.C. International*, November 25–December 15th 1955, Mason Temple, Memphis, Tenn., 14.

63. *Souvenir Journal, Women's International Convention C.O.G.I.C., Leadership Conference Silver Anniversary Addition*, San Francisco, Calif., May 1975.

64. *The Whole Truth*, Volume XIV, No VI, COGIC Headquarters, Memphis, Tenn., June 1981, 7.

65. Lillian Brooks Coffey, quoted in Moore, *Celebrating the Homegoing*, Disk 1.

66. Glenda Williams Goodson, *Mother Elizabeth Juanita (Eula) Dabney*, in Louis F. Morgan, "The Flame Still Burns," *Charisma* (Nov. 2007): 50

67. Elizabeth Juanita Dabney, *What It Means to Pray Through* (Memphis, Tenn.: COGIC Publishing Board 1987, rpt. 1991), 36–37.

68. Ibid.

69. Emily Bibby, quoted in Icy D. Gines, *One Day at a Time, Memoirs of Madam Emily Bram Bibby* (Kearney, Neb.: Morris Publishing, 2007), 5, 16.

70. Mother Larry Fields, quoted in "Christian Women Sharing the Church's Task," *Souvenir Journal Thirty-Second annual Women's International Convention of the C.O.G.I.C., Inc.*, Detroit, Michigan, May 11–16, 1982, 90.

71. Reatha Morris, quoted in Jacqueline Landrum-Sanderlin, *Reflections of the Life and Times of Dr. Reatha Morris D. Herndon* (Los Angeles, Calif.: J.L.S. Publishing, 2005).

72. Fannie Page, quoted in *Souvenir Journal of the 55th Annual Convention*, 35.

73. Annie Lee Stamps, quoted in Church of God in Christ, *50 Years of Progress in California*, 52.

74. Ibid.

75. Mrs. Boyd, quoted in *Souvenir Journal, 55th Annual Convention*, 38.

76. *Souvenir Journal Church of God in Christ, 74th International Holy Convocation*, November 3–13, 1981.

77. Glenda Williams Goodson, *Whole Truth*, Leadership Conference Special Preview Edition, Delegation from the United Kingdom, January 1997.

78. Ibid.

79.Glenda Williams Goodson, *Royalty Unveiled*, 244–52.

80. Lillian Brooks Coffey, quoted in Moore, *Celebrating the Homegoing*, Disk 1.

81. *The Whole Truth*, October 1978, 4.

82. *The Progressive Youth*, A Quarterly Magazine of the COGIC, Published in the interest of the National and State Y.P.W.W. and Sunday School, Volume 14, Fourth Quarter 1944, Number 4, Elder S.A. Jordan, Editor, 811 West 25th Street, Houston, Unit 8, Texas, 5–6.

83. *National Souvenir Journal of the Forty-fifth Annual Convocation Churches of God in Christ*, Mason Temple, November 25–December 14, 1952, 29.

CHAPTER 7: SEEKING THE JUST SOCIETY

1. C. Eric Lincoln and Lawrence Mamiya, *The Black Church in the African American Experience* (Durham, N.C.: Duke University Press, 1990), 11–16.

2. Larry Murphy argues that in the priestly/pastoral approach of "social quietism–accommodation to negative social circumstances...[o]ne might also see it as enabling a people living in seemingly intractable hostile conditions to carve out of the chaos a space of survivability." See "All Things to All People," in *Down by the Riverside: Readings in African American Religion*, ed. Larry Murphy (New York: New York University Press, 2000), 137–38.

3. August Meier, *Black Leaders of the Nineteenth Century* (Champaign, Ill.: University of Illinois Press, 1991).

4. Benjamin Quarles, *The Negro in the Making of America* (New York: Macmillan Publishing Co., 1969), 126.

5. Ibid., 148.
6. Ibid., 149.
7. Ibid.
8. There is a discrepancy within the literature related to the year of Mason's birth. The date that appears in most of the literature is September 8, 1866 (See Elnora Lee, *C.H. Mason: A Man Greatly Used of God*; Mary Mason, *The History and Life Work of Elder C. H. Mason and His Co-laborers* (1924) 1987; Charles Pleas, *Fifty Years Achievement from 1906–1956* (1957) 1991. The year 1862 is based upon the personal oral testimony of Mason's daughter Lelia (Tiny) Mason Byas (see tape recording, Historical Cultural Museum and Fine Arts Center, "The Life and Times of Bishop C. H. Mason" by Lelia Mason Byas) and the date published on Mason's funeral bulletin. A more recent and reliable date is 1864, which is derived from census data (see Chris Brennan's essay). I have chosen 1864 based upon the 1870 census data taken in April of 1870. At that time young Mason was 5 years old.
9. Mechal Sobel, *Trabelin' On: The Slave Journey to an Afro-Baptist Faith* (Westport, Conn.: Greenwood Press, 1979), 99–101.
10. Albert Raboteau, "Preface," Clifton H. Johnson, *God Struck Me Dead: Voices of Ex-slaves* (Cleveland: Pilgrim Press, 1993), xxii.
11. Sobel, *Trabelin' On*, 4.
12. James Evans, Jr., *We Have Been Believers: An African American Systematic Theology* (Minneapolis: Fortress Press, 1992), 40.
13. Ibid., 40–41.
14. Leon F. Litwack, *Been in the Storm So Long* (New York: First Vintage Books, 1979), 122.
15. Robert Franklin notes that during the post-Reconstruction period the majority of Black churches advocated a pragmatic accommodationist position in their quest for social equality. See *Another Days Journey: Black Churches Confronting the American Cities* (Minneapolis: Fortress Press, 1997), 44.
16. Mason was well known for his prayer life. One member remembers that Mason often prayed, "A better day Lord, a better day." Interview with Nadine Granger, July 5, 2001
17. C.P. Jones, "A Message of Hope for the Black Man: How He May Get Thro [sic] This Awful Time," *Truth*, 3 December 1903.
18. Ibid.
19. Peter Paris, "The Bible and the Black Churches," in *The Bible and Social Reform*, ed. Edward Sandeen (Philadelphia: Fortress Press, 1982).
20. Ibid.
21. From Acts 17:26–30. Quoted from Bishop Louis Ford in video, *The Story of Bishop C.H. Mason and the Development of the Church of God in Christ* (Memphis: Church of God in Christ Publishing Board, 1993.
22. It is said that Mason governed the church with "plenipotentiary" powers, exercising unlimited authority over the direction of the church.

23. Juanita W. Faulkner and Raynard D. Smith, eds., *It Is Written: The Church of God in Christ Book of Minutes, 1919–1933* (in press) explicitly documents Holt's involvement in the church and attests to the status that Whites achieved in the denomination. Also see Joe Maxwell, "Building the Church," *Christianity Today*, April 8, 1996.

24. Mary Mason, *The History and Life Work of Bishop C.H. Mason* (Memphis: Church of God in Christ Publishing House, 1987), 32.

25. Ibid.

26. Ibid.

27. Falkner and Smith, eds., *It Is Written.*

28. See Clemmons, *Bishop C.H. Mason*, 53; David D. Daniels, "Everybody Bids You Welcome: A Multicultural Approach to North American Pentecostalism," in Murray W. Dempster, et al., *The Globalization of Pentecostalism: A Religion Made to Travel* (Irvine, Calif.: Regnum Books, 1999).

29. The full story of the nature of this relationship has yet to be told. For a detailed account of the Assemblies of God involvement in COGIC, see Vinson Synan, *The Holiness-Pentecostal Movement in the United States* (Grand Rapids, Mich.: William B. Eerdmans Publishing Company, 1971), 169–70.

30. Letter written by August Feick, April 6, 1926, used by permission of Flower Pentecostal Heritage Center.

31. Ibid.

32. Daniels, "Everybody Bids You Welcome," 229.

33. Douglas J. Nelson, "For Such a Time as This: The Study of Bishop William J. Seymour and the Azusa Street Revival" (Ph.D. diss., University of Birmingham, 1981), 206.

34. Ithiel Clemmons, "True Koinonia: Pentecostal Hopes and Historical Realities," in *Pneuma: The Journal of the Society for Pentecostal Studies* (Spring 1982): 53.

35. Letter written by August Feick, April 6, 1926.

36. Daniels, "Everybody Bids You Welcome," 229.

37. James Delk, *He Made Millions of People Happy* (Hopkinville, Ky.: privately printed, 1945), 7

38. Mason, quoted in Jerry Ramsey, *The Late Apostle C.H. Mason Speaks* (n.p., n.d.), 14–16.

39. Ibid., 16.

40. Quoted from Bishop Louis Ford in video, *The Story of Bishop C.H. Mason.*

41. Clemmons, "True Koinonia," 53.

42. Mason, quoted in "An Appeal to Ride the Railroads," *The Whole Truth*, April, 1931, italics mine.

43. Mason, *The History and Life Work of Bishop C.H. Mason*, 36–40.

44. Quoted from Bishop Louis Ford in video, *The Story of Bishop C.H. Mason and the Development of the Church of God in Christ.*

45. The sight of Black men in official U.S. uniforms troubled many Whites, and the idea that Black soldiers might meet White women in France as social equals created a hysteria. See Kornweibel, "Bishop C.H. Mason and the Church of God in Christ During World War I: The Perils of Conscientious Objection," in *Southern Studies* 26 (Fall 1987): 265.

46. Ibid.

47. J. William Harris, "Etiquette, Lynching, and Racial Boundaries in Southern History: A Mississippi Example," *American Historical Review*, issue, no. 60 (April 1995): 399.

48. Kornweibel, "Bishop C.H. Mason and the Church of God in Christ During World War I," 275.

49. Ibid.

50. Ibid.

51. Kornweibel, "Bishop C.H. Mason and the Church of God in Christ During World War I," 277.

52. Mason, *History and Life Work*, 33-34.

53. Interview with Nadine Granger, July 5 , 2001.

CHAPTER 8: "A MORE EXCELLENT WAY"

1. Albert Outler, ed., *John Wesley* (New York: Oxford University Press, 1964), vii; Arthur Skevington Wood, "The Contribution of John Wesley to the Theology of Grace," in *Grace Unlimited*, ed. Clark Pinnock (Minneapolis: Bethany Fellowship, 1975), 210; Fisher Humphreys, "Baptists and Their Theology," *Baptist History and Heritage* (Winter 2000); also see Ithiel C. Clemmons, *Bishop C. H. Mason and the Roots of the Church of God in Christ* (Bakersfield, Calif.: Pneuma Life Publishing, 1996); Anthea D. Butler, *Women in the Church of God in Christ: Making a Sanctified World* (Chapel Hill, N.C.: The University Press of North Carolina, 2007); Calvin White Jr., *The Rise to Respectability: Race, Religion, and the Church of God in Christ* (Fayetteville, Ark.: The University of Arkansas, 2012).

2. James Cone, *Spiritual and the Blues* (Maryknoll, N.Y.: Orbis Press, 1972); Peter Paris, *Social Teachings of the Black Church* (Minneapolis: Fortress Press, 1985); Cheryl Sanders, *Saints in Exile* (New York: Oxford University Press, 1996); Leonard Lovett, *Black Holiness-Pentecostalism: Implications for Ethics and Social Transformation* (Ph.D. Diss., Emory, 1978) {appears the Lovett doc got dropped; need to reinsert}; Donald Dayton, *The Theological Roots of Pentecostalism* (Grand Rapids, Mich.: Baker Academic, 1987); Frank Macchia, *Baptized in the Spirit: A Global Pentecostal Theology* (Grand Rapids, Mich.: Zondervan, 2006); Douglas Jacobsen, *Thinking in the Spirit: Theologies of the Early Pentecostal Movement* (Bloomington & Indianapolis: Indiana University Press, 2003).

3. Mary Mason, *The History and Life Work of Elder C.H. Mason, Chief Apostle, and His Co-Laborers* (n.p., 1924; rpt. 1987), 19, 20.

4. Joanna P. Moore, *In Christ's Stead: Autobiographical Sketches* (Chicago: Women's Baptist Home Mission Society, n.d.), 43.

5. Lloyd A. Olson, *Eternal Security: Once Saved Always Saved* (Mustang, Okla.: Tate Publishing, 2007).

6. Edward M. Brawley, ed., *The Negro Baptist Pulpit: A Collection of Sermons and Papers by Colored Baptist Ministers* (Freeport, N.Y.: Books for Libraries Press, rpt. 1971 [orig. pub. 1890]); Mechal Sobel, *Trabelin' On: The Slave Journey to an Afro-Baptist Faith* (Westport, Conn.: Greenwood Press, 1979).

7. Lowell Barks Sr., et al., *Glorious Heritage: The Gold Book, Documentary-Historical, Church of the Living God, Motto (CWF) 1899–1964* (n.p., 1967), 22; William Christian, *Poor Pilgrim's Work* (Texarkana, Ark.: n.p., 1896), 14.

8. John M. Giggie, *After Redemption: Jim Crow and the Transformation of African American Religion in the Delta 1875–1915* (New York: Oxford University Press, 2008), 166.

9. Described in Barks, *Glorious Heritage*, 17.

10. Mason, *History and Life Work of Elder C.H. Mason*, 23–25.

11. John H. Green, "Introduction," in Charles Price Jones, *An Appeal to the Sons of Africa* (Jackson, Miss.: Truth, 1902), xiii; Charles Price Jones, *The Gift of the Holy Spirit in the Book of Acts: A Series of Sermons* (Jackson, Miss.: circa 1910), 24; Dale T. Irvin, "Charles Price Jones: Image of Holiness," in *Portraits of a Generation: Early Pentecostal Leaders*, edited by James R. Goff Jr. and Grant Wacker (Fayetteville, Ark.: The University of Arkansas Press, 2002), 37–50.

12. Charles Price Jones, quoted in David Douglas Daniels III, "The Cultural Renewal of Slave Religion: Charles Price Jones and the Emergence of the Holiness Movement in Mississippi" (Union Theological Seminary, New York, Ph.D. diss., 1992), 146–47; Irvin, "Charles Price Jones: Image of Holiness," 46; Daniels (1992), 146-147.

13. O.B. Cobbins, ed., *History of the Church of Christ* (Holiness) U.S.A. 1895–1965 (New York: Vantage Press, 1966), 28–29.

14. On political hope, see Jones, *Truth* (15 May 1906), cited in Daniels (1992), 201; on the justice of God and the redemption of Africa, see Jones, "An Appeal to the Sons of Africa" in *An Appeal to the Sons of Africa* (Jackson, MS: Truth, 1902),

15. Jacobsen, *Thinking in the Spirit*, 77.

16. "1916 Minutes of the General Assembly of the Church of God in Christ," excerpts, in Lucille Cornelius, *The History of the Church of God in Christ* (n.p., 1975), 53; Eugene B. McCoy, "'Yes, Lord' Historical Account of Charles H. Mason and the Church of God in Christ" (n.p., n.d), 33.

17. Justus Bowe, "The Church," in Mary Mason, *The History and Life Work of Elder C.H. Mason, Chief Apostle, and His Co-Laborers* (n.p., 1924; rpt. 1987), 72–73.

18. William B. Holt, comp., *A Brief Historical and Doctrinal Statement and Rules for Government of the Church of God in Christ* (n.p., circa 1917), 13.

19. Ibid.

20. Ibid.

21. Ibid.

22. "Minutes of the General Assembly, Church of God in Christ, 10 December 1928" (private collection of Juanita Faulkner, West Windsor, N.J.).

23. "Minutes of the General Assembly, Church of God in Christ, 10 December 1924" (private collection of Juanita Faulkner, West Windsor, N.J.).

24. Ibid.

25. O. T. Jones Sr. and J. E. Bryant, eds., *Manual of the Church of God in Christ* (n.p., circa 1933;1951 rev. ed.).

26. Mason, *History and Life Work of Elder C.H. Mason*, 24, 46; "Minutes of the General Assembly-extended session, Church of God in Christ, 5 January 1927" (private collection of Juanita Faulkner, West Windsor, N.J.).

27. Lillian Brooks Coffey, compiler, *Year Book of the Church of God in Christ for the Year 1926* (n.p.,circa 1926; rpt. 1990 by Jerry R. Ramsey III), 25–26.

28. Mason, *History and Life Work of Elder C.H. Mason*, 5, 49; Holt, *Brief Historical and Doctrinal Statement*, 9.

29. Jones and Bryant, *Manual of the Church of God in Christ*, 5–6.

30. Ibid., 49.

31. See ibid., 41–62.

32. Mason, *History and Life Work of Elder C.H. Mason*, 31.

33. Coffey, *Year Book of the Church of God in Christ for the Year 1926*, 29–31.

34. Mason, *History and Life Work of Elder C.H. Mason*, 46.

35. Jones and Bryant, *Manual of the Church of God in Christ*, 56–57.

36. Mason, *History and Life Work of Elder C.H. Mason*, 40–44.

37. Ibid., 53.

38. Ibid., 19.

CPSIA information can be obtained
at www.ICGtesting.com
Printed in the USA
LVHW052328290122
709396LV00005B/23